Called to Live
the Dynamic Power of the Gospel

SFO Resource Library

Called to Live the Dynamic Power of the Gospel

COMMENTARY ON THE RULE OF THE SECULAR FRANCISCAN ORDER

by

PHILIP MARQUARD, OFM

Franciscan Press

Called to Live the Dynamic Power of the Gospel
Philip Marquard, OFM

Franciscan Press
Quincy University
1800 College Avenue
Quincy, IL 62301
217.228.5670
FAX 217.228.5672

Book design and typesetting by Laurel Fitch, Chicago, IL.

Printed in the United States of America
First Printing: December 1998
1 2 3 4 5 6 7 8 9 0

Library of Congress Cataloging-in-Publication Data
Marquard, Philip, 1912 or 14-1986.
    Called to build a more fraternal and evangelical world : commentary
on the Rule of the Secular Franciscan Order / by Philip Marquard.
        p. cm. -- (SFO resource library : vol. 3)
    Includes bibilographical references and index.
    ISBN 0-8199-0977-7 (pbk. : alk. paper)
    1. Secular Franciscan Order. Regula Ordinis Franciscani Saecularis.
2. Secular Franciscan Order--Rules. I. Title II. Series.
BX3652.M 1997
255'.3--dc21   97-6548
                                                                       CIP

Contents

T

Foreword

T Called to Build a More Fraternal and Evangelical World began as a series of commentaries on the Rule of the Secular Franciscan Order which appeared in the Franciscan Herald magazine between 1979 and 1980. These articles have been slightly edited in accordance with the passage of time and are now able to be presented in book form.

This text is the fruit of long experience and depth of vision. The author, the late Fr. Philip Marquard OFM who passed away in 1986, had been a shining light on the Secular Franciscan scene for well over 30 years with his monthly articles in the Franciscan Herald, with his many years of service on the national level in SFO organization and government, with his untiring efforts at spiritual assistance for numerous fraternities with the Secular Franciscan Province of the Sacred Heart (USA), and with his involvement of many Secular Franciscans in his various outreach projects to aide and give dignity to the poor, marginalized, and homeless. He knew the theory. He knew the practice. He lectured and preached about the gospel way for Secular Franciscans, and he had enabled the seculars to actualize their commitment through many types of apostolic involvements from a right-to-life telephone hotline to a soup kitchen in downtown Chicago to a halfway house for ex-offenders.

His commentaries on the Secular Franciscan Rule were born of this rich blend of matured insight and concrete action. He spoke from the heart, but he also spoke to the practical situations of life. He applied the Gospel to the signs of the times and interpreted life's daily experiences from the perspective of "the words, the life, and the teaching and the Holy Gospel" of Jesus Christ (cf. 1221 OFM Rule, 23:41).

Through his commentary on the Secular Franciscan Rule, the "dynamic power of the Gospel" (SFO Rule,7) comes alive and takes on a persuasive force. By means of this book, Fr. Philip's service and assistance to the Secular Franciscan Fraternity challenges every member and everyone who animates and guides the communities to take seriously and to make effective the call of the SFO Rule to go "from Gospel to life and life to the Gospel" (Art. 4).

Benet A. Fonck OFM

Introduction:
The Foundations on which the Rule is Built

T The Rule of the Secular Franciscan Order is not a new rule, but an up-to-date version of the original rule or Franciscan Way of Life for Secular Franciscans. It is the expression of the ideals of St. Francis in a practical manner according to the norms set forth in the Second Vatican Council.

The original rule for Secular Franciscans drawn up by St. Francis is no longer extant. He perhaps wrote this rule in 1209 or 1210. Cardinal Hugolino, the Protector of the Franciscan Order and close friend of St. Francis, took the original short rule of St. Francis and, in 1221, set it up in more legal form. This rule was approved orally in that year by Pope Honorius III.

In the following decades, considerable confusion arose about the Third Order Rule because of the divergent local versions that came into existence and also because of the addition of various local customs. As a result, in 1289, Pope Nicholas IV issued a universally uniform rule that remained in force until Pope Leo XIII adapted it to more modern conditions in 1883. This rule of Leo XIII was supplemented by the General Constitutions approved in 1957.

This new version of the rule approved by Pope Paul VI is the result of sifting through the various temporary versions of the rule which Secular Franciscans accepted after considering the rule in the light of the Second Vatican Council. In the United States, for example, there was a temporary version of the rule accepted by all the Third Order Provinces. Now, with this present version of the rule approved by Paul VI, we have a universal rule for all Secular Franciscans.

It is well to remember as we study this new version of the rule that it is a Way of Life and not merely a series of legal prescriptions. We know that St. Francis designated the Gospel as the supreme norm of life. He meant to put the Gospel before and above all conventionalism and every human law. Consequently, St. Francis resisted binding the lives of his followers with too specific prescriptions, for fear that the gospel principles be given secondary importance or that they be restrained by the limits of the letter of the law. So the rule is to be a guide that opens to the vastness of the gospel challenge. If we observe all of the regulations of the rule, we are not truly following Francis. We must merely use the rule as a stepping stone to the Gospel and its ideals. It is then that we will really attain a true union with Christ.

Besides this open-ended quality of the gospel challenge, we must also have a grasp of the charism or moving force of St. Francis' life if we are to understand properly, and apply authentically, the Rule of the Secular Franciscan Order.

At the close of his life, St. Francis distinguished two periods in his life. The early part of his life he described very frankly and concisely as "when I was in sin," the latter part as "when I did penance," that is, "when I changed my heart and really sought God." The Franciscan historian Fr. Cajetan Esser wrote: "The beginning of this 'doing penance' is in the obedience he gives to God's command which urges him to the care of lepers. Accordingly, in the life of the saint, the period of sin, of disobedience to God, and the period of penance, of obedience rendered to God ever anew, stand opposed to each other. He no longer did what he wanted himself but what God demanded of him: 'that which seemed bitter to me.' In the process, he came to experience a special grace, that his bitterness was 'changed into sweetness of soul and body.' Penance to him is thus the conversion of a person from a life centered on the personal 'I' to a life which is completed under the will and sovereign lordship of God. Thus, penance is the same as 'change of heart' in the biblical sense ('Turn away from your sins and believe in the good news,' Mk 1:15), and according to the mind of St. Francis, it must be the basic life attitude of all his followers."

St. Francis always saw the life of penance as being under the leadership of obedience. This is seen from his words: just as the beast of burden "does not go along the road properly without the rod of correction, so it is for the body of the penitent." Every penitent needs correction to remain on the path of God. So the person who possesses the spirit of penance discovers it's easy and sweet to fulfill the commandments of God. The life of penance or change of heart is clearly the essence of the spirit of St. Francis. It is a prerequisite of our ability to live the Franciscan way of life.

In the beginning of his Testament, St. Francis describes the path of his personal vocation in these words:

> "This is how God inspired me, Brother Francis, to embark upon a life of penance. When I was in sin, the sight of lepers nauseated me beyond measure; but God himself led me into their company, and I had pity on them. When I had once become acquainted with them, what had previously nauseated me became a source of spiritual and physical consolation for me. After that, I did not wait long before leaving the world."

"Doing penance" is the central concept for beginning a truly Christ-like life which demands an actual break with the "world" and total conversion to God. Francis, however, was so convinced of the constant need to renew this "beginning," this "doing penance," that even near the close of his life, he said to his followers: "Let us begin, brothers, to serve the Lord God because so far, we have made little or no progress in anything."

This "doing of penance" under the grace of God prepared Francis for the decisive revelation of the will of God for him. It was to live his life according to the form of life of the Holy Gospel.

When St. Francis heard the gospel passage on the feast of St. Matthias in 1209, in which Jesus sent his apostles to preach the Gospel without money, knapsack, shoes, or spare tunic (Mt 10:1-42), he immediately cried out enthusiastically: "This is what I wish, this is what I seek, this is what I long to do with all my heart."

The Gospel remains inert words if it is not lived. St. Francis took recourse to the Gospel to illuminate his life, but he also projected life into the Gospel, asking of it the answer to his human needs. As his biographer Thomas of Celano said,: "Francis' highest intention, his chief desire, his uppermost purpose was to observe the holy Gospel in all things and through all things, and, with perfect vigilance, with all zeal, with all the fervor of his heart, to follow the teaching and the footsteps of our Lord Jesus Christ."

It is well for us to remember the gospel life can never be confused with a commentary on the Gospel or even with a mystical interpretation of its words. It is a life of faith and of obedience to the living Lord. It is essentially a sincere and unconditional surrender of self to Christ as a Person, not a theology or a system. Behind the text of the Gospel, we must see the Person of Christ pointing out the need of evangelical conversion.

Therefore, we must read, reflect, and meditate on the Gospel. Only with this prayerful attitude will we ever be able to conform our lives to the Gospel.

Fr. Cajetan Esser stated very emphatically: "Something very important, perhaps even decisive, is here expressed about the original intention of St. Francis. He was not concerned primarily with some kind of external activity in the service of the Church perhaps, nor in any pressing way with the realization of this or that virtue as the first principle of the Order; neither was he concerned with ideals of some kind or another, but with a *life*, or rather, with *the life* according to the form of the Gospel which the Almighty himself had revealed to him and which the Lord Pope had approved for him to live by."

If we want to follow Francis, we must understand these two concepts of his life: doing penance and living according to the form of the Gospel. It is these two central concepts that we must see in this new version of the rule and strive to make them basic in our daily living. Living according to the form of the Gospel became, through St. Francis, a principle of formation as well as the first and highest duty of the whole Franciscan movement.

chapter one

The Prologue
of the Rule

T The 1978 version of the rule for Secular Franciscans utilizes as a prologue a summary of the "Letter to All the Faithful" written by St. Francis. It will be interesting to see what impact this letter has on present members and, particularly, on new members.

CONTENTS OF THE LETTER TO ALL THE FAITHFUL

Actually, the Rule was not written by St. Francis, but the "Letter to All the Faithful" was. So the new version of the rule offers these words of St. Francis. There are some authorities on Franciscanism who think this was the first rule for lay followers of St. Francis.

The "Letter to All the Faithful" consists of two parts: "Those who do penance" and "Those who do not do penance." The first part is very encouraging, bringing out the importance of the love of God and our union with Christ, closing with the priestly prayer of Christ spoken at the Last Supper, begging for unity of all with his Father.

The second portion is quite severe with open threats of damnation, being slaves of the devil, "damn his soul," and being eaten by worms. These statements may turn people off unless they are carefully explained and not isolated from the mercy of a loving heavenly Father. The entire gospel message must be taken into consideration to fully understand these references to Christ's words.

One thing we must bear in mind is that St. Francis wished to portray the whole Christ, not just the "fair-haired boy side." The Christ of the Gospels also expressed indignation against his own disciples when they did not understand the things of God. To Peter on one occasion, he said: "Get behind me, Satan." On another occasion, he made a whip and drove money-changers out of the temple.

Christ said: "I was born for this, I came into the world for this: to bear witness to the truth." He never sought human approbation. This truth of Christ was known in the Old Testament by the Hebrew word "emeth" and is, in Jewish thinking, the reliability of God's love. Christ lived only for this, to make us realize the truth that we are loved by God and that this love is to be relied upon no matter what we may do. God loves us as we are, and he always does so: "We may be unfaithful, but he is always faithful, for he cannot disown his own self" (2 Tim. 2:13).

Yet Christ speaks straight from the shoulder, as to the Pharisees: "You are whitened sepulchers, beautiful without but full of dead men's bones within"; or "Depart from me you cursed into everlasting fire prepared for the devil and his angels." Christ makes it clear: "Enter by the narrow gate since the road that leads to perdition is wide and spacious, and many take it; but it is a narrow gate and hard road that leads to life, and only a few find it" (Mt 7:13-14). So if we speak about a broad way, we are not speaking about the Gospel.

Christ, however, understands human weakness. He is infinitely kind as only God can be. This we see in his parable of the Prodigal Son, or the Good Shepherd, or his words on the cross: "Father, forgive them."

St. Francis had a grasp of the whole Christ even though the words he used in the second portion of his letter seem to cloud this. Hence, we must read and interpret this letter in light of the whole Gospel, the whole Christ.

THE PURPOSE BEHIND THE LETTER TO ALL THE FAITHFUL

The very purpose of St. Francis' letter is to bring about a change of heart for the person who reads it. He called his Franciscan Third

Order the Order of Penance. The word "penance" comes from the Greek word "metanoia" which means change of heart.

Father Peter van Breemen, SJ expresses this in the following way: "Strange as it may sound, there is required a true 'metanoia' before man or woman can allow himself or herself to be loved by God. This is one of the most profound paradoxes of the human situation, for as on the one hand everyone yearns for this love of God and yet it requires a fundamental change of mentality before a man can let the love of God really flow into his life. There is something in us which shrinks from being receptive. We all have a strong tendency to be autonomous, to control our own lives, and in so doing, to make ourselves happy. 'Metanoia,' that word which scripture uses so often, means a deep, personal reorientation to God, a change in my priorities and values, in my actions and reactions; it is really an existential transformation reaching into the depths of my being. This 'metanoia' is vital, for the man or woman who does not let himself or herself be loved by God makes his or her life a sterile thing."

Christ's first sermon as reported in the first chapter of St. Mark is an invitation to repent and believe the Gospel. And then St. Mark immediately tells us how the first apostles repented and believed the Gospel. Simon and Andrew heard the invitation and "left their nets" to follow Christ. James and John, "leaving their father Zebedee in the boat," followed Christ. If one, therefore, is really to repent and believe the Gospel, one has, in some way, to renounce selfishness.

True faith presupposes repentance: "Repent and believe the Good News." Before we can accept this tremendous gift of the Good News, we must change, for without this transformation, our life will remain sterile. Scripture constantly insists that anyone's sterility comes from his or her closing self off from God's love.

Repenting and believing the Gospel is not something that is done once and for all. That is why each year, at the beginning of Lent, placing ashes on our foreheads, the Church's priests say to each of us baptized persons: "Repent and believe the Gospel." Repenting and believing need a constant renewal. This is also the reason why St. Francis gave lay people a rule to live by as they follow in his footsteps to Christ.

We must constantly be careful that we do not live the Gospel in such a way that it does not appeal to others. If we make the Gospel too ordinary, too mediocre, we cannot arouse the enthusiasm or interest of others. The rule is given to us to be certain that we are not distorting Christ or his Gospel. Hence, the exhortation and warning of St. Francis in his "Letter to All the Faithful" to have a worthy setting before the rule itself.

We are always to show our faith in the Good News and express the values that the Gospel contains in our every day life by joyfully making whatever sacrifices are necessary.

chapter two

A United Franciscan Family

T 1. The Franciscan family, as one among many spiritual families raised up by the Holy Spirit in the Church, unites all members of the People of God—laity, religious, and priests—who recognize that they are called to follow Christ in the footsteps of Saint Francis of Assisi.

In various ways and forms but in life-giving union with each other, they intend to make present the charism of their common Seraphic Father in the life and mission of the Church.

2. The Secular Franciscan Order holds a special place in this family circle. It is an organic union of all Catholic fraternities scattered throughout the world and open to every group of the faithful. In these fraternities, the brothers and sisters, led by the Spirit, strive for perfect charity in their own secular state. By their profession, they pledge themselves to live the Gospel in the manner of Saint Francis by means of this rule approved by the Church.

3. The present rule, succeeding "Memoriale Propositi" (1221) and the rules approved by the Supreme Pontiffs Nicholas IV and Leo XIII, adapts the Secular Franciscan Order to the needs and expectations of the Holy Church in the conditions of changing times. Its

interpretation belongs to the Holy See and its application will be made by the General Constitutions and particular statutes.

The first article of the Secular Franciscan Rule immediately establishes the relationship of the Secular Franciscans with the entire Franciscan Family. This, of course, is of paramount importance to the very Franciscan existence of the Secular Franciscans as a vital part of the Franciscan Family. The Secular Franciscans are not the dog's tail wagging in the rear but are true and full members of St. Francis' Family. They were raised up by the Holy Spirit in the Church with other members of our Franciscan Family.

The Secular Franciscans are called to follow Christ in the footsteps of St. Francis as lay persons in the world in life-giving union with all the other members of our Franciscan Family. They, like the other dedicated members of our Franciscan Family, "make present the charism of their common Seraphic Father in the life and mission of the Church."

WHAT ABOUT CHARISM?

Charism is a word that has been used a great deal in recent years in the Church. It is important to understand what it really means. Charism is a general term that indicates a personal gift of the Spirit used for the good of the Church. When it is approved by the Holy Father, the charism is said to participate in the official mission of the Church to make Christ present in the world. St. Francis sought this approval for his charism as soon as he possibly could. The first reaction of the Holy See was great hesitancy. The pope and cardinals thought he was seeking to do too much. What he desired was to live out the Gospel life of Christ. But all finally realized that if they denied his request, they would be saying that the real life of Christ as brought out in the Gospel was impossible to imitate.

Actually, almost all true charisms at first blush run into some opposition one way or the other. The Holy Spirit gives a faithful person a charism when he opens himself or herself to grace. As Fr. Lazaro Iriarte de Aspurz OFMCap writes in his book, *The Franciscan Calling*, "A charism of election is given to do a great work for the good of the whole Church. Generally, the opportunity is the conversion: a radical and painful turning point in life. We think of

St. Anthony Abbot, St. Benedict, St. Francis, St. Ignatius, St. John of God, St. Teresa Avila, St. Collette, and others. At least, the Spirit usually puts every founder to the hard test of anticonformity; the majority have seemed strange or unusual to their contemporaries. Simultaneously, there is a profound evangelical experience, full of light and confidence, and the call to leave everything to order one's life in conformity with the light that has been received. The charism opens the way, with progressive strength, urging the chosen one to carry to others the benefits of his own discovery. He feels a vital need to communicate the gift he has so freely received (cf. 1 Cor. 9,16). The kind of life begun by the converted one, his example, his action and, more than anything, the sincerity and inspiration that vibrate in his words, are for men and women of sincere heart a kind of new promulgation of the Gospel, a new vision of the Gospel, perhaps, of an aspect particularly demanded by the historical moment."

St. Francis was very particular about keeping his charism intact. We can see this from the incident which occurred after his return from the Holy Land to Italy in the spring of 1221. He was very disappointed with the changes that had been made by some of his followers. He repudiated large and permanent friaries, monastic observances, and difficult fasts inconsistent with alms-gathering and walking the gospel trail carrying the good news to others.

One day, he climbed to the roof of a large friary and started to remove the shingles as if to begin its demolition. He was especially unhappy with written privileges that led to pretentiousness and caused some of the brothers to forget about their vital duty of witnessing to the Gospel and its suffering servant Christ.

The charism of St. Francis was simply to live the Gospel of Our Lord Jesus Christ. Anyone called by grace to do this and admitted by the proper authority into any of the Three Orders of St. Francis belongs to our Franciscan Family.

THE FAMILY OF FRANCIS

Secular Franciscans are called by grace to embrace the charism of St. Francis. They are admitted and professed according to the Rule of St. Francis as approved by the proper authority. So Secular Franciscans share in the full Franciscan Family Life.

St. Francis was very interested in all people and in the world
God created. It was his desire to bring the spirit of Christ into the
secular world. Among the steps he took to realize this was the
founding of his third order, the Secular Franciscan Order. He knew
that men and women who improve the world and continue the
work of creation would sanctify the universe as part of their service
to God. He wished that people living in the world would be strong in
faith, hope, and love so they would be effective instruments for
Christ and his work. As a result, he was happy to found a third order
for the men and women who sought to follow his charism in the
midst of the world.

That Secular Franciscans have understood this charism and
participated fully in the Franciscan Family is readily seen from
many who have been recognized by the Church as Blessed and
Saints. They have come from all social ranks, families and careers,
royalty and peasants, martyrs and penitents, lawyers and businessmen, parents and youth, physicians and blacksmiths. They touched
the lives of many people of the world and left a telling mark on the
lives of many. Several founders and foundresses of other religious
institutes began as Secular Franciscans and then enriched the
Church with their great ideals.

Hence, besides participating in the charism of St. Francis,
Secular Franciscans participate in the complete spirit of our
Franciscan Family. This includes its spirituality, community, apostolic ministries, and simple life style. Though they are not religious,
they share Franciscan life as seculars, people living in the world but
not of the world. They complement and complete the expression of
the Franciscan charism. Therefore, they are authentic members of
our Franciscan Family.

Franciscans of the three orders of St. Francis are commissioned
to promote family life among the members of the various orders.
This is done, first of all, by thoroughly understanding that we are all
members of the one Franciscan Family. With our appreciation of
our call to this Franciscan way of life, our enthusiasm grows; and we
extend ourselves to one another in mutual charity, understanding,
and patient service. At times, all can pray and worship together. On
occasion, a meal or recreation can be shared. There has always been
some participation in common apostolic undertakings. And, today,
there are ministries that are on a more continuous basis as, for

instance, the interaction of the First Order with committed lay volunteers of the Third Order in foreign and domestic undertakings for God's people.

Therefore, the first article of the Secular Franciscan Rule is on target when it states: "The Franciscan Family, as one among many spiritual families raised up by the Holy Spirit in the Church, unites all members of the people of God—laity, religious, and priests—who recognize that they are called to follow Christ in the footsteps of St. Francis of Assisi."

chapter three

The Gospel Way

T 4. *The rule and life of the Secular Franciscans is this: to observe the Gospel of our Lord Jesus Christ by following the example of Saint Francis of Assisi, who made Christ the inspiration and the center of his life with God and people.*

Christ, the gift of the Father's love, is the way to him, the truth into which the Holy Spirit leads us, and the life which he has come to give abundantly.

Secular Franciscans should devote themselves especially to careful reading of the Gospel, going from Gospel to life and life to the Gospel.

5. Secular Franciscans, therefore, should seek to encounter the living and active person of Christ in their brothers and sisters, in Sacred Scripture, in the Church, and in liturgical activity. The faith of Saint Francis, who often said, "I see nothing bodily of the Most High Son of God in this world except his most holy body and blood," should be the inspiration and pattern of their eucharistic life.

The meat of the Secular Franciscan Rule was always the second chapter on the way of life. With this new version of the rule, it is still just that. The second chapter opens in declaring that the very essence of this way of life is the observing the of our Lord Jesus Christ according to the spirit of St. Francis.

KNOWING CHRIST THROUGH THE GOSPEL

Francis found Christ in the Gospel. Christ was actually present there for him. It was in the Gospel that he learned about the details of Christ's life from his humble birth to his sacrificial death and glorious resurrection. He entered so much into the reading of the Gospel that the narratives about Christ became living realities to him. This led him to re-enact many features of Christ's life, as the birth at Greccio, his solitude in the hillside, heralding the Good News similar to a troubadour, and entering into the love and sacrifice of Calvary on Mount Alverna.

The love of Christ so enamored Francis that he spent whole nights saying: "Love is not loved." He felt badly that many did not grasp Christ's tremendous love for mankind.

If you read the Book of Hosea in the Old Testament, you get some idea of how Francis felt about Christ. The prophet Hosea possessed a love for his wife which was a human expression of God's love for his people. Though his wife was unfaithful and lived as a prostitute, he did the incredible thing of loving her despite her weakness and sinfulness. It caused him much anguish; but he struggled to love her nevertheless until he won her back. The covenant of the Old Testament uniting God and Israel was so intimate that it was marriage. When Israel was unfaithful and broke that covenant, it was adultery and divorce.

Francis understood that the new covenant, sealed in the blood of Christ, is no less real and serious. When we are unfaithful to the covenant, we are adulterers and prostitutes.

Christ marries us even though he knows our weakness. We are unreliable lovers since we let ourselves be swayed by many things. We give him so many reasons to abandon us; but he never does. Like Francis, we can read in the Gospel the marvelous extent of Christ's love. It is unconditional and absolute, bestowed upon Peter who denied him, Thomas who doubted, Mary Magdalene, and the good thief on the cross. Christ forgives any sorrowful sinner now matter how far he has fallen. His love is absolute.

When we grasp Christ's great love for us, then we can say we know him. It is the Gospel that enables us to do just this.

For example, one of our Franciscan businessmen on the Board of the former St. Anthony Inn (a halfway house for ex-offenders in Chicago) died in the late 1970s. He truly understood what real Christian love is. He was completely devoted to God, his Church, his wife, family, fellowmen, and, particularly, the unfortunate. His complete unselfishness gave him a great serenity of mind and heart which all could sense when they were in his company. He would never talk about himself; but he worked diligently for the needs of others. He lost his wife after 15 years of marriage and later married again, spending 50 wonderful years with his second although she was eventually confined to a wheelchair. God gave him 94 years of active life, though practically all of his friends thought he was only in his 70s. Then in a mere three weeks, leukemia brought his warm and gentle life to an end. While he was in the hospital, he was very cheerful and interested in knowing about everyone. His wife was brought to the hospital in her wheelchair, and she would sing a love song to him which expressed the tremendous love between them. He was such a caring person, and she expressed her appreciation so vividly.

Our love can also catch some of the characteristics of Christ's love if we enter deeply into knowing Christ in the Gospel as Francis urges us.

LIVING THE GOSPEL

Francis desires that we live the Gospel, make it our way or rule of life. Hence, he would never want his own human rule to replace the Gospel. All it was meant to do was to urge his followers to accept the challenge of the entire Gospel. Francis would not have us observe some regulations set down by him and then let us fall into the trap of feeling good about ourselves. No. His very words: "Let us begin because up to now, we have done nothing," indicate very clearly that the entire Gospel is always before us.

As a result, Thomas of Celano, St. Francis' first biographer, wrote: "His rule is made up of crumbs from the Gospel." Then he went onto say: "When Blessed Francis saw that the Lord God was daily adding to their number, he wrote for himself and his brothers, present and to come, simply and with few words, a form of life and rule, using for the most part the words of the Holy Gospel, for the perfection of which alone he yearned. But he did insert a few other things that were necessary to provide for a holy way of life."

Hence, we see that the life of a follower of Francis cannot have any other norm or rule than the Gospel itself. And Francis pointed out very precisely how we are to live the Gospel. He desired that the gospel precepts and counsels be understood as our Lord gave them and not as the worldly wisdom and prudence of men and women would like to interpret them. Thomas of Celano wrote: "Francis' highest intention, his chief desire, his uppermost purpose was to observe the holy Gospel in all things and through all things and, with perfect vigilance, with all zeal, with all the longing of his mind and all the fervor of his heart, to follow the teaching and the footsteps of our Lord Jesus Christ."

Due to the weakness of our human nature and our poor response to grace, at times, we do have a real struggle walking in the sandals of Francis. They just don't fit us too readily. But he does not worry about our clumsy progress as long as we are plodding along. In fact, it is just this plodding that will eventually open our minds and hearts to new gospel horizons.

This brings to my mind a Secular Franciscan who died a few years ago. He had all the material blessings of this world and was detached from them. At the height of his career, he contracted cancer. His first reaction was frantically to go here and there to the best doctors. But all disappointed him with the same verdict of doom. Then he rose to the occasion, drank deep from the Gospel, and said that he wished to cheerfully suffer all of the pangs of his cancer for his sins. When death did come, he could go straight to God. This he did.

If we read the Gospel in a spirit of prayerful humility, we will find Christ in the Gospel and be inspired to follow his way of life. Our intention must be to put into practice what we read and not feel proud because we know something about the Gospel.

chapter four

Fidelity to the Church

T 6. *They have been made living members of the Church by being buried and raised with Christ in baptism; they have been united more intimately with the Church by profession. Therefore, they should go forth as witnesses and instruments of her mission among all people, proclaiming Christ by their life and words.*

Called like Saint Francis to rebuild the Church and inspired by his example, let them devote themselves energetically to living in full communion with the pope, bishops, and priests, fostering an open and trusting dialogue of apostolic effectiveness and creativity.

In the spirit of St. Francis, the new version of the rule in Article Six requires a Secular Franciscan to be a loyal, faithful, and constructive member of the Catholic Church. This is a firm command and is also the only gateway through which anyone can enter the family of Francis.

FAITH THE BASIS OF OUR ATTITUDE

Love of the Church is one of St. Francis' great characteristics which flowed from his faith. The famous Protestant historian Paul

Sabatier wrote a life of St. Francis; and, in his book, he makes this statement:

> "St. Francis' great originality was his Catholicism.... The Church was his spiritual home, and he had become fully aware that every instance of progress in his spiritual life was sealed with the mark of the Church. He was conscious of making progress; but he was conscious, too, that the Church awaiting him at every turn in the road to renew his desire, replenish his strength, and chart his course for still further progress. He, more than anyone else, felt indebted to the traditional influence (of the Church)—indebted to it but not its slave. It acted, and he acted; and his own activity was, as it were, the fruit of this two-fold influence... Again, it would be absurd to make of Francis a revolutionary or a man who was unconsciously Protestant; yet it would be no less so to picture him as an echo, pure and simple, of authority—or a man who had renounced his own conscience."

St. Francis looked upon the Church as the bride of Christ, and he loved the Church as he loved Christ. The Church was also, for him, Christ extended into every day life. He wanted his three Orders to live in the very heart of the Church and to partake of its life.

In the *Legenda Antiqua* of St. Francis, we read this statement of his: "From the beginning of my conversion, the Lord spoke to me through the mouth of Bishop of Assisi to counsel me and strengthen me in the service of God. When I think of this and of the high dignity of the superiors of the Church, I want to love, respect, and regard as my superiors, not only bishops but even the poorest priests."

Although St. Francis was a reformer and an innovator, he never put himself in a position to be at odds with the Church. Truly, he recognized the human deficiencies of the Church; but he always remained humble and discreet, holding fast to his faith, love, and respect for the Church. Francis had a very vital faith that was at the root of his great loyalty. While other reformers left the Church to do their work, he was convinced of the utter nonsense of dropping out of the living Body, the Church, under the pretext of curing its illness. He knew that a branch cut off from the living tree dies, and he was too thrilled with the life of Christ to leave its source.

St. Francis' chief concern was to remain in vital union with the

Church, to think, believe, live, and "feel" with the Church. He had a true Catholic sense. This, he stated in his Second Rule for the First Order: "that we may be utterly subject and submissive to the Church. And so, firmly established in the Catholic faith, we may live always according to the poverty, and humility, and the Gospel of our Lord Jesus Christ, as we have solemnly promised." As a result, he was a real builder and repairer of the Church, renewing its spirit and life. This is what he expects of us.

FIDELITY OUR BADGE

When Pope John Paul II was in Mexico in 1979, he invited the Mexicans and all of us to a strong and intelligent fidelity to the Church. He cited the fidelity of Mary as an example of our fidelity to the Church and explained the four dimensions of this fidelity.

The first dimension is searching. Mary was faithful when she searched for the profound meaning of the will of God in her life. She asked the angel at the annunciation, "how might this be possible?" There can be no fidelity if there is not this deep-seated searching, when we cannot find in the heart of man the answer which only God has. Hence, to be faithful to the Church, we must always strive to know her better. Pope John Paul suggested we read the Vatican II Document on the Constitution of the Church (*Lumen Gentium*) and study it with loving attention. There, he says, we will discover that today there is not a "new Church." The Second Vatican Council has revealed with more clarity the one Church of Christ, one having new magnitude or scope but the same essence.

The second dimension of the fidelity we are called upon to have is acceptance. Mary said, "let it be, or behold the handmaid of the Lord; be it done unto me." In other words, she was willing. This is the moment of truth for fidelity, the moment in which we come to realize that we can never fully understand the "why," that there are in God's design more areas of mystery than explanations; that no matter how hard we try, we will never be able to accept everything. At that moment, then, we are ready to accept this mystery and give it a place in our hearts, as Mary kept all these things in her heart. It is the moment in which we open ourselves to this mystery, not in the way someone gives up facing an enigma or the absurd, but rather with the openness of someone letting himself be possessed by something—someone—bigger than his heart. This acceptance is fulfilled through faith which is the union of our being with the mystery that is revealed.

Pope John Paul II stated that he expects of us a loyal acceptance of the Church. He added that we cannot be faithful and remain attached to secondary things, valid in the past but already outdated. We will not be faithful either, he went on to say, if we try to build the so-called Church of the future, unrelated to the present. We must be faithful to the Church born once and for all from the plan of God: at the cross, the empty tomb, and at Pentecost, which was born not of the people or from reason, but from God. She is born today to build among all men and women a people willing to grow in faith, home, and fraternal love.

The third dimension of fidelity given by the Holy Father is coherence, which means to live in accordance with what one believes. We must adjust our lives to what we adhere to. This demands of us that we accept misunderstanding and persecutions rather than break with what we believe in. There must never be a break between life and convictions. That is coherence. Here, we find, perhaps, the most intimate nucleus of fidelity.

This coherence implies an awareness of our identity as Catholics, giving public witness to it. We need only think of the remarkable example of St. Thomas More, a Secular Franciscan, who sacrificed his life rather than compromise himself. Today, the Church needs us to give witness to our faith and share in the Church's mission in the world, being the ferment of faith, justice, and human dignity, in order to build a more human and fraternal world from which we can look up to God.

The fourth dimension of fidelity is perseverance. As Pope John Paul II pointed out, it is easy to be faithful for a day or a short time. But it is difficult to be loyal through an entire life of faith. The "fiat" of Mary at the annunciation found its fulfillment in the "fiat" at the food of the cross. She persevered in her fidelity to Christ through his hours of disgrace, mistreatment, and cruel death.

We are called upon, with the help of grace, to continue and deepen our coherence in our faith in Christ's Church. Open persecution may not be our lot, but there is always the possibility that our perseverance can be tested by indifference, misunderstanding, and neglect. Pope John Paul II stated: "Do not lose your enthusiasm for 'being the Church,' for you must begin everyday anew with greater fervor and strength." It reminds us of St. Francis' words: "Let us begin because up to now we have done nothing." We need this spiritual resiliency to be always faithful, loyal, and instrumental in building up the life and activity of the Church. This is what the new version of the rule implies in the sixth article where it reads: "Secular Franciscans have been united more intimately with the Church by Profession."

Our Change of Heart

T *7. United by their vocation as "brothers and sisters of penance," and motivated by the dynamic power of the Gospel, let them conform their thoughts and deeds to those of Christ by means of that radical interior change which the Gospel itself calls "conversion." Human frailty makes it necessary that this conversion be carried out daily.*

On this road to renewal, the sacrament of reconciliation is the privileged sign of the Father's mercy and the source of grace.

Stagnation, we know, is unhealthy for water and for people. We must move, flow towards Christ. St. Francis, following the spirit of the Gospel, called it penance, which (in the biblical sense) means a change of heart. It is an ongoing process in which we must be involved.

RADICAL INTERIOR CHANGE

The new version of the rule in Article Seven asks the Secular Franciscans to "conform their thoughts and deeds to those of Christ by means of that radical interior change which the Gospel itself calls 'conversion.' Human frailty makes it necessary that this conversion be carried out daily." It is only too clear that there is no instant transformation into Christ. When you speak about a radical interior change, you are necessarily speaking about a change that will be arduous, illusive, and demanding.

St. Peter calls upon all of us to "be like newborn babies, always thirsty for the pure spiritual milk, so that by drinking it, we may grow up and be saved" (1 Pet 2:2). It takes time to grow up, and there are many pitfalls and much stumbling along the way.

If we have any doubts as to what we must change in order to accomplish a radical change, St. Peter suggests: "Do your best to add goodness to your faith; and to your goodness add knowledge; to your knowledge add self-control; to your self-control add endurance; to your endurance add godliness; to your godliness add brotherly love; and to your brotherly love add love. These are the qualities you need, and if you have them in abundance, they will make you active and effective in your knowledge of our Lord Jesus Christ. But whoever does not have them is so shortsighted that he cannot see and has forgotten that his past sins have been washed away" (2 Pet 1:5-9).

In a letter to all the priests throughout the world issued in the late '70s, Pope John Paul II insisted upon the necessity of being converted anew each day. He rightly called it a fundamental exigency of the Gospel addressed to everyone. "Being converted," he wrote, "means returning to the very grace of our vocation; it means meditating upon the infinite goodness and love of Christ, who has addressed each of us and, calling us by name, has said: 'Follow me.'"

Pope John Paul puts this into practical words when he stated that being converted means continually "giving an account" before the Lord. There is first the giving an account of our hearts about our service, our zeal, and our fidelity, for we are Christ's servants. Then we must give an account of our negligences and sins; of our timidity, of our lack of faith and hope, of our thinking only "in a human way" and not "in a divine way." Here, we need only think of St. Peter who objected when Christ said he must suffer and die. "God forbid it," he cried out, "this must never happen to you!" Jesus turned around and said to Peter: "Get away from me, Satan! You are an obstacle in my way, for these thoughts of yours are men's thoughts, not God's" (Mt 16:22-23).

Another point that Pope John Paul recommends is that in being converted, there is implied seeking again the pardon and strength of God in the sacrament of reconciliation. The new version of the rule in Article Seven puts the same directive in this rather stilted manner: "On this road to renewal, the sacrament of reconciliation is the privileged sign of the Father's mercy and the source of grace." A prudent and consistent use of this sacrament assists us greatly in our renunciation of self and our growth in the love of Christ and others. It is the best way to learn the habit of giving cheerfully for God loves a cheerful giver. "Each one should give, then, as he had decided, not with regret or out of a sense of duty; for God loves the one who gives gladly" (2 Cor 9:7).

A final practical suggestion on what being converted means, Pope John Paul insists, is to pray continually and never lose heart. In his words, prayer, in a certain way, is the first and the last condition for conversion, spiritual progress, and holiness. It is prayer that shows the essential style of our lives; without prayer, this style becomes deformed. Prayer helps us always to find the light that has led us since the beginning of our Franciscan vocation and which never ceases to lead us, even though it seems at times to disappear in the darkness. Prayer enables us to be converted continually, to remain in a state of continuous reaching out to God, which is essential if we wish to lead others to him. Prayer helps us to believe, to hope, and to love, even when our human weakness hinders us.

THE "SPIRIT OF THE LORD"

St. Francis always made it clear that despite all our efforts, the real growth in Christ in our lives is due to the Spirit of the Lord. This is evident if we just look at his testament in which he used so often the phrases "the Lord gave me" or "the Lord revealed to me," thus showing that everything comes from God. As Fr. Cajetan Esser wrote: "Francis also knew that the outer man must decay day by day, that the inner man may be renewed. Francis placed great stress on both these elements of the spiritual life: God's initiative and our reply. He insisted that each of us play one's role fully if our life of renunciation is to attain its profound objective. Only if each is allowed one's full scope, will growth be possible for the evangelical person, the 'new' man or 'new' woman, the citizen of the kingdom of God, whose heart and mind belong wholly to the Lord. The man or woman filled with the Spirit of the Lord no longer seeks comfort in himself or herself, in living a purely selfish life. In freedom, in detachment from self and the world, in the limpid purity of a heart wholly open to the Spirit of God who fills all and quickens all, there is consummated in its fullness the evangelical life of repentance."

It is this abundance of life springing from the Spirit of the Lord that explains st. Francis' zeal in following Christ. He did not merely imitate Christ externally, nor merely follow his example. Francis was open wide to the supernatural life of Christ, living as a vital branch on the vine.

Francis ignored the quibbling and the distinctions flowing from the wisdom of the world. He got himself out of the way and went straight ahead following out the directives of the Gospel. His fidelity was absolute; he neither discussed nor hesitated. All was to be according to the Gospel. Because of this generosity and openness, Jesus gave him immediately the fullness of what, for others, is reserved to the future.

So many of the followers of St. Francis imitated his method of spiritual formation and established a conversion of heart and mind that won them much peace and joy. We can readily point to St. Margaret of Cortona, the Franciscan Mary Magdalene. The change of heart that she achieved was truly due to her openness to the Spirit of the Lord. From a worldly, selfishly sexual woman, she grew to know the great joy of the intimacy of pure love in a supernatural union with Christ. Today, after 700 years, her body is still preserved incorrupt. All the result of a magnificent change of heart.

St. Francis never gave any detailed instruction for the concrete circumstances of anyone's life. He much preferred to inculcate basic attitudes rather than give details directives and programs. Out of love for God and his kingdom, Francis urged his followers to deny themselves in the spirit of the Gospel and to work to overcome harmful desires. But how we are to realize this ideal in our personal lives, he preferred to leave to God's inspiration. Hence, he avoided any narrow regulations which might well hinder the free working of grace.

To attain a true change of heart as the seventh article of the rule directs, it is, therefore, necessary for all of us to give full prominence to the primacy of God's love in our hearts. Nothing human or material must stand in the way of that love.

chapter six

The Rule Speaks about Prayer

T *8. As Jesus was the true worshipper of the Father, so let prayer and contemplation be the soul of all they are and do.*

Let them participate in the sacramental life of the Church, above all the Eucharist. Let them join in liturgical prayer in one of the forms proposed by the Church, reliving the mysteries of the life of Christ.

In Article Eight, the Rule of the Secular Franciscans confronts you with the importance of prayer in your life. Prayer is really a precondition for your effective living of the gospel life.

A FRANCISCAN TRADITION

St. Francis set his eyes on the example of Christ in his practice of prayer, and he urged his followers to do the same. From the time St. Francis discovered God as his Father, he developed a heart-to-heart contract with God whom he came to know in prayer. His constant life of prayer is the best explanation of the spiritual success of his life.

Hence, St. Francis instructed all of us to keep close watch over ourselves or we will turn our minds and hearts from God because we think there is something worth having or doing or that we will gain some advantage. To quote his words from the First Rule: "In the love which is God, I entreat all my friars, ministers, and subjects, to put away every attachment, all care and solicitude, and serve, love, honor, and adore our Lord and God with a pure heart and mind; this is what he seeks above all else. We should make a dwelling-place within ourselves where he can stay, he who is the Lord God Almighty, Father, Son, and Holy Spirit."

St. Francis did not arrive at his spirit of prayer easily. He passed through various stages of purification. There was first of all his frustration at Spoleto and the distaste for worldly pleasures. He sought relief in prayer in cares and particularly at San Damiano's where the voice from the crucifix spoke to him. Then, when he was disinherited by his earthly father, he turned fully to his heavenly Father. "How glorious, how holy and wonderful it is to have a Father in heaven" (Letter to All the Faithful). Finally, we see him on the night with Bernard of Quintavalle. He was completely immersed in prayer as he repeated "My God and My All." His own unworthiness was known to him, and he marvelled at the richness and goodness of God his Father. On LaVerna, he climaxes these prayerful thoughts: "Who are you, my sweet Lord, and who am I, your useless and miserable servant?"

As a result of his deep union with God his Father and Christ his Brother, St. Francis found that everything he saw and did became for him an occasion to think of God and speak to him. Everything in nature lifted his thoughts to God. All things became invitations to him to praise God and find joy in having such a wonderful God who created so many beautiful inanimate and animate things.

In the same way, all the events of his life were not due to chance or luck but he saw the provident hand of God his Father behind all of it. He had the habit of opening up the Gospel when he desired to know God's will for him. In this same fashion, he acted when he dealt with Bernard of Quintavalle and others.

The late Pope John Paul I wrote many letters to various individuals. In 1974, which was the seventh hundred centenary of St. Bonaventure's death, he wrote a letter to this great Franciscan saint. St. Bonaventure had been a professor at the University of Paris, minister general of the Franciscan Order, a cardinal, an orator, member of the Ecumenical Council of Lyons, and he wrote many books. Pope John Paul I asks in this letter what was really the outstanding achievement of St. Bonaventure's life. He said that he would choose his biography on the life of St. Francis, and that he would spread its knowledge everywhere. The late Pope stated that, when one reads this life of St. Francis, his spirit is profoundly moved. "We have a saint writing about a saint." This great spiritual fruit of St. Francis springs from his intimate union with God in prayer.

YOUR DAILY PRACTICE

St. Francis' spirit of prayer has been captured by thousands of his followers. It is also open to you. With an openness to grace and deeper understanding of St. Francis' spirit, you will make the progress you desire. As St. Paul wrote: "Whether, then, you eat or drink, or do anything else, do everything for God's glory" (1 Cor. 10:31). So prayer should pervade all your activities and leisure, your joys and your sorrows.

The oft-repeated words of St. Francis, "No one showed me what to do but the Most High Lord himself," indicate his deep union in prayer with God. His equally close relationship with our Eucharistic Christ is telling evidence of his prayerful hours with Christ. Hence, he urged us every time we enter a church to pray: "We adore you, O Lord Jesus Christ, here and in the churches throughout the world, and we praise you because by your holy cross you have redeemed the world."

As a result of this attitude of St. Francis and the whole spirit of the Church, the rule states: "Let them participate in the sacramental life of the Church, above all the Eucharist." St. Francis found much strength and inspiration from the Eucharistic Sacrifice. Today, many people are still struggling to understand the new liturgy and feel at home in it. The lack of mystery and reverence in may expressions of some liturgies does find them wanting in the minds and hearts of many. The evident lack of respect in the houses of God, the open talking, the ignoring of Christ in the tabernacle, and the casual behavior of worshippers does grate on the spiritual sensitivities of many. All this should not make you beg off or grow lukewarm. Your own interior spirit of faith must grow stronger and exert a proper stimulation for interior growth in others. Good liturgies are around us, and we should support them. Holy Mass must still be our main act of worship. Here, Christ is our priest, our victim, and our food. St. Francis was insistent upon clean churches, clean linens, and the utmost respect for the Eucharist. Your supportive help is necessary today. We must always keep in mind his deep reverence for the priest, even an unworthy one, because the priest changes the bread and wine into the body and blood of Christ.

The next most important prayer for a secular Franciscan is the daily liturgical office. The rule reads: "Let them join in liturgical prayer in one of the forms proposed by the Church, reliving the mysteries of the life of Christ." The fact that you are called upon to say some form of liturgical prayer each day emphasizes your special vocation as a member of the Secular Franciscan Order. It raises you to greater dignity and brings out the vitality of your role as a true and loyal supporter of Christ's Church.

When you say a liturgical office, you do not merely pray as an individual but as an official spokesperson for the Church. This form of prayer has more efficacy and is supported by the whole Church. Though you may, at first, feel weak and humble, your liturgical prayer helps you to realize your tremendous potential for good.

Thomas of Celano, the biographer of St. Francis, wrote that St. Francis preferred the divine office, the Church's official prayer, to every other prayer. He recited it with particular care and devotion. When he was ill, he would ask one of his brothers to read it to him.

There are various liturgical offices available to you. Any reputable Catholic bookstore would carry the Liturgy of the Hours in its full or shortened versions. There is also the updated version of the Office of the Blessed Virgin; perhaps, the best is the Liturgy of the Hours with the special supplement of the Franciscan feasts, available through various Franciscan supply centers. There are many others. It is well to use one that appeals to you.

The essential part of the liturgical office is the Morning Prayer and the Evening Prayer. Neither is too long to discourage you if you ordinarily have a busy day. Each can be easily prayed in about eight minutes. Anyone who has the time will also find the other parts of the liturgical office rewarding. To be considered liturgical, an office must consist of a hymn, psalms, a reading from Holy Scripture, prayers of intercession, and an official prayer of the day.

Other forms of prayer and private devotions are surely meant to be a daily part of a Secular Franciscan's life. The rosary, holy hours, the way of the cross, approved novenas, and the like are very helpful for the spiritual and human growth of everyone. Sound private prayer is necessary for every follower of Christ. The value of wholesome charismatic prayer opens some to particular graces and greater joy.

When we cultivate a deep spirit of prayer in our lives, we will find that it is a tremendous strength in our moments of trial and discouragement. It brings prayer to our hearts and lips even when we may not be fully conscious. This was clear in the last months of the life of a father and husband in the Northwest Franciscan Community in Arlington Heights, Illinois. He was in a coma in the hospital for many weeks. On a visit to his bedside on one occasion, a Japanese woman, who was keeping vigil at her husband's bedside in the same room throughout the night, told me, referring to our Secular Franciscan: "He is a very good man. During the night he speaks so confidently and loving to God. He is in deep union with God." It was a spontaneous prayer coming from a man who had learned long ago how to speak intimately to God.

Something we must keep in mind is that prayer is a grace which must be sought for with perseverance: "Lord, teach us how to pray!" At the same time, we must not forget that our own constant effort is necessary for success in prayer. The inspiration that flows from each of us can be a big factor in spurring all of us on in our life of prayer.

chapter seven

Mary in the Rule

T *9. The Virgin Mary, humble servant of the Lord, was open to his every word and call. She was embraced by Francis with indescribable love and declared the protectress and advocate of his family. The Secular Franciscans should express their ardent love for her by imitating her complete self-giving and by praying earnestly and confidently.*

One of the new features of the revision of the rule is the special attention given to the Blessed Virgin Mary. This is an authentic expression of the Marian spirit of St. Francis and every Franciscan.

MARY IN THE RULE

The rule asks Secular Franciscans to express ardent love for Mary by imitating her complete self-giving and by praying earnestly and confidently. Self-giving is a real characteristic of Christ, and Mary learned it well. It is a difficult task for anyone of us to achieve, but is something we must daily strive to acquire. This article of the rule indicates how Mary became a self-giving person. "She was the humble servant of the Lord open to his every word and call." With this openness to grace, we, too, can find it possible to imitate her as the rule requires.

Veneration and imitation of Mary is a Franciscan tradition. The part Our Blessed Lady played in the actual formation of St. Francis' inner spirit is recorded by St. Bonaventure, where after telling the story of the reading of the gospel passage on the feast of St. Matthias and how St. Francis found his new vocation in the reading, he relates: "Now Francis, the servant of God, abiding in the church of the Virgin Mother of God, with continuous sighing besought her that she would deign to become his advocate; and by the merits of the Mother of mercy, he did himself conceive and give birth to the spirit of gospel truth as Mary has conceived the word full of grace and truth."

St. Francis' devotion to Mary sprang from his gospel orientation. We are told he was attached to her "with an ineffable love because she gave us the Lord of majesty as our brother." He also loved her because poverty was reflected brightly in her. He wrote to St. Clare and instructed her to follow the life and poverty of our Lord Jesus Christ and his Blessed Mother.

Hence, is it any wonder that he dedicated special prayers to her as, for example, his salutation of the Blessed Virgin Mary and the antiphon to the office of the passion. St. Francis had a deep love of the Portiuncula Chapel dedicated to our Lady of the Angels. His love of Mary and his desire for spiritual joy resulted in our Franciscan Crown of the Seven Joys of Mary. Love leads to devotion. Therefore, all Franciscans, like Francis, who have ever had a tender love of Mary seek to imitate her Christlike virtues.

Sound devotion to Mary is rooted in the Bible. There we see that Mary had a vital role in salvation history. She shared in the three periods of salvation history: the age of expectation, the age of fulfillment, and the age of glorification. In the age expectation, she was a true daughter of Israel awaiting the coming of the Messiah with ardent faith. In the age of fulfillment, she was the obedient daughter of God at the annunciation where she said, "Behold the handmaid of the Lord," and remained faithful to her commitment at the very foot of the cross of redemption. In the age of glorification, she shared in the birth of the Church on Pentecost and also in the resurrection of Christ through her assumption into heaven.

SOLID DEVOTION TO MARY

These Biblical roots of Mary give rise to solid devotion to Mary.

In his 1979 historical visit to Poland, Pope John Paul II evinced a great esteem and love of Mary. A copy of Jasna Gora's famed black madonna was making a tour of all the parishes of Poland since it was blessed by Pope Pius XII in 1957. While Pope John Paul was in Poland, this statue had arrived in the diocese of Czeztochowa, and he was filled with joy about it.

On that occasion Pope John Paul said: "This visit has given tangible expression to the teaching of the Second Vatican Council that is contained above all in the Dogmatic Constitution of the Church. These visits have shown what is the real maternal presence of the mother of God in the mystery of Christ and of his Church. Going forth form her shrine in Jasna Gora to visit each diocese and each parish in Poland, Mary has shown herself to all of us in a special way as our mother. For a mother does not merely wait at home for her children; she follows them wherever they stay. Wherever they live and work or form their families, wherever they are pinned to a bed of pain, even on whatever path they have strayed, where they are forgetful of God and weighed down by guilt. There a mother follows her children, everywhere."

Later, Pope John Paul asked these questions: "Was not the moment of the annunciation in Nazareth a great turning point in the history of mankind? Did not Mary bring hope to the house of Zechariah when she went to visit her kinswoman Elizabeth? In our difficult times, did not Pope Paul VI call the mother of God the beginning of a better world? Did not Blessed Maximilian Kolbe (a Franciscan), the Polish 'Knight' of the Immaculate, also feel the same mystery?... I wholeheartedly bless those who welcome Mary."

Mary is indeed our hope and our strength as the renowned prayer, the "Memorare," brings out so clearly. "Remember, O most gracious Virgin, that never was it known that anyone who fled to your protection, implored your help, or sought your intercession was left unaided."

CALLS TO MARIAN DEVOTION

Pope Paul VI, in 1974, wrote an apostolic exhortation, "Marialis Cultis," for the right ordering and development of devotion to the Blessed Virgin Mary. He began with these words: "From the moment when we were called to the See of Peter, we have constantly striven to enhance devotion to the Blessed Virgin Mary, not only with the intention of interpreting the sentiments of the Church and our personal inclination but also because, as it is well know, this devotion forms a very noble part of the whole sphere of that sacred worship in which there intermingle the highest expressions of wisdom and of religion and which is therefore the primary task of the people of God." Pope Paul then proceeded to give a very sound explanation and history of devotion to Mary.

There were two practices of devotion in honor of Mary which Pope Paul VI particularly advocated. These are the Angelus and the Rosary. The Angelus is of Franciscan origin, being attributed to St. Bonaventure. Both the Angelus and the Rosary should be part of our daily lives.

All of the Bishops of the United States issued a beautiful, instructive Pastoral Letter on the Blessed Virgin in 1973, entitled "Behold Your Mother." They called attention to the lack of interest in Marian devotions and devotions to the saints. They quoted Father Karl Rahner in relation to his: "When he was asked about the decline of Marian devotion, the German Jesuit, Father Karl Rahner, declared that the special temptation that affects Christians today, Catholics and Protestants alike, is the temptation to turn the central truths of the faith into abstractions, and abstractions have no need for mothers."

In this pastoral letter, the bishops clearly stated: "We Bishops of the United States wish to affirm with all our strength the lucid statements of the Second Vatican Council on the permanent importance of authentic devotion to the Blessed Virgin, not only in the liturgy, where the Church accords her a most special place under Jesus her Son, but also in the beloved devotions that have been repeatedly approved and encouraged by the Church and that are still filled with meaning for Catholics. As Pope Paul has reminded us, the rosary and the scapular are among these tested forms of devotion that bring us closer to Christ through the example and protection of his holy Mother."

It is certainly evident that Mary must share in our daily lives. It was a pleasure for me to see a beautiful statue of Mary on the front lawn of a Methodist church in Fort Worth, Texas. Mary desires to lead all of us to Christ, and Franciscans should be in the foreground to help her.

chapter eight

Speaking of the Gospel Counsels

T 10. United themselves to the redemptive obedience of Jesus, who placed his will into the Father's hands, let them faithfully fulfill the duties proper to their various circumstances of life. Let them also follow the poor and crucified Christ, witnessing to him even in difficulties and persecutions.

11. Trusting in the Father, Christ chose for himself and his mother a poor and humble life, even though he valued created things attentively and lovingly. Let the Secular Franciscans seek a proper spirit of detachment form temporal goods by simplifying their own material needs. Let them be mindful that according to the Gospel, they are stewards of the goods received for the benefit of God's children.

Thus, in the spirit of "the Beatitudes," and as pilgrims and strangers on their way to the home of the Father, they should strive to purify their hearts from every tendency and yearning to possession and power.

12. Witnessing to the good yet to come and obliged to acquire purity of heart because of the vocation they have embraced, they should set themselves free to love God and their brothers and sisters.

The Rule of the Secular Franciscan Order covers the three evangelical counsels of poverty, chastity, and obedience in Articles 10, 11, and 12. Secular Franciscans are expected to live in the spirit of these counsels even though they do not pronounce vows. The counsels have been called the marrow of the Gospel since they are so necessary for a more fruitful life in Christ. They are a powerful means of increasing the divine life within ourselves.

THE SPIRIT OF OBEDIENCE

Our real purpose in life is to do God's will. We are called upon to listen to his voice and say with Samuel of the Old Testament: "Speak, Lord, your servant Samuel listens."

Christ called our attention to the need to listen to God's commands and directives any number of times. You remember the following incident recorded by St. Luke: "Now as Jesus was speaking, a woman in the crowd raised her voice and said, 'Happy the womb that bore you and the breasts you sucked!' But he replied, 'Still happier those who hear the word of God and keep it'" (Lk 11:27-28). Christ's response is a far greater praise of Mary than the woman in the crowd had given. Christ reinforces the tribute to his mother: Do not bless her because of something physical, but rather because she heard the Word of God and has kept it and lived for it.

On another occasion, Christ's mother and his apostles were searching for him; but they could not reach him because of the crowd. He was told, "Your mother and brothers are standing outside and want to see you." But he said in answer, "My mother and my brothers are those who hear the word of God and put it into practice" (Lk 8:19-21). We know that no one heard the word of God more than Mary; she opened herself completely to it. At the same time, no one put it into practice more than she: through her, it became flesh. If you look closely, you will note that in the verse in the Gospel before this one, Jesus had warned: "Take care how you hear." Mary is the perfect example of how to hear. "I am the handmade of the Lord, let it be done unto me" (Lk 1:38).

God looks for this openness and receptivity in all of us. It is only then that he can truly be God and do wonders for us. So obedience demands generosity on our part. The story is told of a king who, when he was being crowned, was presented gifts by his new subjects. They were rich and beautiful. But one poor man came who had no gift. Kneeling before the king, he said simply and sincerely: "I give you myself." No other gift could be compared to it. No greater gift can be given than that of giving life. True obedience to God becomes a holocaust, a whole burnt offering, and is received by God as "an odor of sweetness." By this very fact, we become a consecrated offering, set aside for the divine worship.

Such a spirit of obedience aids us in following the poor and crucified Christ. We see the need and have the means then of overcoming any critical spirit, and we strive to rise above murmuring to find the joy of living in union with God.

THE SPIRIT OF POVERTY

Article 11 of the rule treats the spirit of poverty which meant so much to St. Francis as he viewed the humble and poor Christ in the Gospel. On one occasion, the brothers asked St. Francis by what virtue we become dearest to Christ. He answered as if laying bare the secret thought of his heart: "You know, brothers, that poverty is a special way of salvation, being, as it were, the food of humility and the root of perfection. For poverty is that treasure hidden in the field of the Gospel, which to buy, a man would sell all he had, and the things which cannot be sold are to be desired in comparison therewith" (St. Bonaventure's Life of St. Francis). "This is the sublimity of the highest poverty which has made you, dearest brothers, heirs and kings of the kingdom of heaven, poor in goods but exalted in virtue. May this be your portion which leads to the land of the living, to which wholly attached, you should desire to possess nothing else under heaven, for the name of our Lord Jesus Christ" (First Order Rule).

The first Beatitude is "how happy are the poor in spirit; theirs is the kingdom of heaven." Of all the Beatitudes, this is the only one in the present tense, all of the others are in the future tense. The poor in spirit have their treasure in heaven, where their Father is, and, hence, even now their heart and their home are in heaven as well. They are filled with a genuine and all-pervading joy, like St. Francis, who was a thoroughly happy man precisely because he was poor in spirit. Just observe and you will note how those who are really poor for the sake of the kingdom seem to radiate a very simple and special joy.

The happiest people you will meet will be those who live their spirit of poverty seriously. Besides, these are also the people who share most readily with others. They are apostles not so much for what they say and do, but by what they are.

This reminds me of the delightful little story of Serapion who sold his book of the Gospels and gave the money to the poor, commenting wryly: "I have sold the book which told me to sell everything that I had and give it to the poor!"

No, we are not called upon to sell everything we have; but we are called upon to live simple lives, not to clutter up our lives with countless material things. Spiritual spring cleaning is always in order especially in our present consumer society. We are to learn to be content with few and poor things. A spirit of detachment must grow within us which enables us to find our true possession in God as St. Francis did: "My God and My All."

In the Franciscan ideal of poverty, the three counsels are embraced in the spiritual sense under the simple idea of poverty. By the spirit of chastity, we leave our sensual inclinations and selfishness and prepare ourselves for union with Christ. By the spirit of poverty we renounce attachment to material things and fulfill a faithful stewardship over what we do have. Finally, by the spirit of obedience we give up our greatest possession, namely, our own will and strive to do the will of God in all things. As a result of good understanding of the spirit of poverty will help us live in the spirit of all the gospel counsels.

THE SPIRIT OF CHASTITY

In Article 12 of the rule, the spirit of chastity is extolled and encouraged. The spirit of gospel chastity calls for purity of mind and heart. It is to enable us to be free to truly love God and all our fellowmen and women. We obligate ourselves to spend our lives manifesting God's love to the world whether we are single or married.

One of the beatitudes states: "Happy are the pure of heart, they shall see God." The single-hearted can and will see God. To be single-hearted means to have no second motives. Such a heart sees God alone. "The lamp of the body is the eye. It follows that if your eye is sound, your whole body will be filled with light" (Mat 6:22).

Like the other counsels, the spirit of chastity is a challenge to us. It does not come easily. When we consider our many shortcomings, the goals we have seem beyond our capacity. This, of course, is true if we limit our view to our own powers. The Gospel is utterly impossible from a natural viewpoint. None of us can follow Christ completely or meet his demands fully. But the worlds of the angel to Mary are likewise true for us: nothing is impossible to God. With such faith, we can build, we can succeed. Of course, mortification on our part is a necessary condition for really seeking God alone, finding single-heartedness.

We know the result when dietary rules are disregarded. True, it is much more difficult to detect spiritual malnutrition, and the consequences are more severe. If a trial or a cross catches you out of condition, it is too late to join the novena circuit and really unsportsmanlike to shout, "Why did God do this to me?" So, we are living dangerously until we realize that our spiritual condition is far more important that social status or financial success.

Today, the ideal of purity is at a low ebb in the secular world. There is an open attack on purity in papers, books, radio, television, movies, and in conversations. Much of the sacredness of sex is lost. Surely we are not to be prudes. But we do need a reverence and a healthy understanding of the goodness of human sexuality. The sacrament of the Holy Eucharist and Communion along with prayer will aid us to maintain such a healthy attitude.

A practical manner of helping ourselves to live in the spirit of the three counsels is to pray the Angelus each day. In the first invocation and response, "The angel of the Lord declared unto Mary and she conceived of the Holy Spirit," we think of Mary's and our own openness to God and detachment from things (spirit of poverty). In the second invocation and response, "Behold the handmaid of the Lord, be it done unto me according to your word," we consider Mary's dedication to doing God's will and our own (spirit of obedience). In the third invocation and response, "And the Word was made flesh and dwelt among us," we reflect on Mary's purity of mind and heart and our own (spirit of chastity). Then, in the prayer that follows, we pray for God's help: "Pour forth we beseech you, O Lord, your grace into our hearts" etc.

chapter nine

One of Many

T 13. *As the Father sees in every person the features of his Son,
the firstborn of many brothers and sisters, so the Secular
Franciscans with a gentle and courteous spirit accept all people as a
gift of the Lord and an image of Christ.*

*A sense of community will make them joyful and ready to place
themselves on an equal basis with all people, especially with the lowly
for whom they shall strive to create conditions of life worthy of people redeemed by Christ.*

*14. Secular Franciscans, together with all people of good will,
are called to build a more fraternal and evangelical world so that the
kingdom of God may be brought about more effectively. Mindful
that anyone "who follows Christ, the perfect man, becomes more of
a man himself," let them exercise their responsibilities competently
in the Christian spirit of serviced.*

Articles 13 and 14 of the rule remind us that no man is an
island. God placed us in this world together, and we have the
responsibility of accepting each other and assisting one another in
true Christian service.

ACCEPTING ALL PEOPLE

It is a tall order to be requested to accept all people, there being so many differences among people. It takes a great deal of grace and an openness to the love of God and others in the spirit of Christ. But we all must try to see how far we can extend ourselves. The thought to remember is that Christ is the firstborn of many brothers and sisters. We are all related in Christ.

St. Francis surely brought this home to us as he embraced all as his brothers and sisters. It was no easy lesson for him to learn as we know when we think of the very fearful and human way he approached the leper. A real grounding in mortification is necessary. We must put aside our personal likes and dislikes.

One modern example of someone achieving this is Donaldi Dolce of Sicily, who has been spending his life for others. He had a bright future as a graduate in architecture besides having influential friends. After he broke his engagement to a lovely girl, the daughter of a wealthy contractor, he kissed his bewildered and protesting mother goodbye as he cut himself loose to work for others. His parents tried to discourage him by saying there was so very much evil and poverty to overcome that one person could do little. To this, he replied: "Someone must begin." You obtain some idea of his Christ-like spirit from the way he filled out his form for his required three months of service in the army. In the space requesting his paternity, he put down God; to the question of how many brothers he had, he entered a billion; and also how many sisters, he wrote a billion. He considered all men and women his brothers and sisters. His reply to the questions of his profession was: "I'm learning to be consumed." He wished to be consumed for others as Christ was, and he felt that in an ordinary lifestyle, he would become fossilized. His desire was to reach out to others in forms of constructive service to make life more Christian.

The rule also suggests that the sense of community called for by our very life of Franciscan brotherhood will give us the joyful readiness to accept all people on an equal basis including even the lowly. Franciscan fraternity life brings all social classes together as brothers and sisters through Christ. All are to enjoy dignity and self-respect.

This spirit within the fraternity must spill over to all people the members encounter. For this reason, we witness Secular

Franciscans befriending and assisting the poor, the alcoholic, the
ex-offender, and many marginal people striving to keep body and
soul together.

A Christian Spirit of Service

Article 14 of the Rule requests that in a spirit of ecumenism, we
work with all people of good will to build a more fraternal and
evangelical world so the kingdom of God may be brought about
more effectively. St. Francis even sought the help of the Sultan in
the enemy camp during the crusades to bring about a better and
more understanding world. He embraced all men and women, asking them to assist in implanting more good will.

The document of ecumenism of the Second Vatican Council
states: "The Council urges Catholics to recognize the signs of the
times and to take an active and intelligent part in the work of ecumenism... Since in our times cooperation in social matters is very
widely practiced, all men without exception are summoned to
united effort. Those who believe in God have a stronger summons,
but the strongest claims are laid on Christians, since they have
been sealed with the name of Christ. Cooperation among all
Christians vividly expresses that bond which already unites them,
and it sets in clearer relief the features of Christ the Servant." As
Franciscans, we are to be particularly aware of this.

Then this article of the rule enjoins us to exercise our responsibilities competently in the Christian spirit of service, which puts us
in the footsteps of Christ who came into this world not to be served
but to serve. Active, practical charity was at all times the way of life
for St. Francis and his followers.

Blessed Luchesio, the first Secular Franciscan, sold his vast
estates and divided the proceeds among the poor. He only retained
for himself and his wife a small piece of property. Regularly, he took
care of the needy, the poor, and the stranded. He would be seen carrying a crippled person on his shoulders. When he was out of sup-
plies, he would take a basket and go from door to door in search of
food for others.

St. Louis IX of France and St. Elizabeth of Hungary, the patrons
of the Secular Franciscan Order, were both outstanding for their
services to the poor and the sick. Besides building hospitals for the
sick, they personally did all they possibly could to help them. When

St. Louis' courtiers murmured about his great acts of service to others, he remarked: "In one way or another, a king is bound to be extravagant; I prefer to be extravagant in almsgiving for the love of God, rather than to be extravagant in worldly and transitory things. In this matter, the immoderate expenditures which often must be made for the sake of worldly undertakings are overlooked and balanced by excess in spiritual things."

To do the task asked of us, we must think big. Our lives are relatively short when we consider all the time taken to nurture and educate us. A Japanese Christian, Toyochiko Kagawa, is a good example of a person who thought big. He said that he had discovered: "That a secret plan is hid in my hand; that my hand is big, big, because of this plan. That God, who dwells in my hand, knows this secret plan of the things he will do for the world using my hand!" He was born in 1888 and was later a convert. To be Christian meant one thing to him: a ministry to the poor. He used the power of the pen to expose slum conditions so vividly that he succeeded in winning support to change some things. He wrote some 565 pamphlets and 50 books. Even though he was sick, he continued his work. In his biography, he is quoted as saying: "With all these ailments, I am still active. Illness is a matter of the spirit. I feel it is half mental and half physical." He did not give himself much rest until God called him to his reward.

In the Gospel, you perhaps remember where Christ in his concern for others touched the man who could neither hear nor speak. He made the man different. We are able to do the same. Not that we can make the dumb speak or the deaf hear. But we can share the pain of others. We can be bearers of forgiveness. We are able to visit the sick and the lonely. Yes, we can make Jesus present to these and many others. Indeed, we must believe that the needs all round us are our obligations. We can do something about some of them. As is always the case, as we help others, we are really also helping ourselves.

The philosopher Albert Camus was invited to address a religious community in France on one occasion. He said: "What the world expects of Christians is that they should speak out, loud and clear, and that they should voice their condemnation of evil and injustice in such a way that never a doubt, never the slightest doubt, could rise in the heart of the simplest man. What the world expects of Christians is that they should get away from abstraction and confront the bloodstained face history has taken on today. The grouping we need is a grouping of persons resolved to speak out clearly and to pay up personally."

Albert Camus is a voice of one speaking from outside the Church. Christ, Francis, and our rule exhort us to do what he expects of a follower of Christ. If we desire to become a spiritual success story, we must come to terms with the words of Christ: "If anyone wishes to rank first, he must remain the last one of all and the servant of all."

chapter ten

Challenges for Your Action

T *15. Let them individually and collectively be in the forefront in promoting justice by the testimony of their human lives and their courageous initiatives. Especially in the field of public life, they should make definite choices in harmony with their faith.*

16. Let them esteem work both as a gift and as sharing in the creation, redemption, and service of the human community.

The rule has some new challenges for us in Articles 15 and 16. From almost a prohibition of active involvement in civil and political concerns in the old version of the rule, we are now challenged to courageous initiatives.

The change is really due to the gradual changes in the official Church. While the pope was a virtual prisoner in the Vatican, action in the public realm was cut off. This influenced all documents emanating from the Vatican as, for instance, the Leonine version of rule under Pope Leo XIII. But when Pope Pius XI signed a concordat with the government of Italy, we hear the call to Catholic Action from the pope. Then, succeeding popes spoke of various types of apostolic action for lay men and women, all culminating in the Second Vatican Council with special documents under the guidance of Pope John XXIII and Pope Paul VI. Then, Pope Paul VI gave us this rule requesting members to individually and collectively be in the forefront of promoting justice by the testimony of their human lives and their courageous initiatives.

JUSTICE AND HUMAN RIGHTS

Human justice is tied very closely to the Gospel. What urges us to respond to others is God's love and visible human need. If our faith and love are genuine, we desire our actions to do more than make us feel good or give temporary relief. We will want our actions to cope with their needs as effectively as possible. To accomplish this, we must push into the public area, into questions of social justice.

With the Gospel as our base of operations, we must want for others rights that we enjoy, a right to a suitable home, job, food, and health care. It should be our goal to overcome situations which violate human dignity. To see others as our brothers and sisters includes our working and praying for their full human dignity as sons and daughters of God the Father and brothers and sisters of Christ.

Christ went about doing good, and St. Francis imitated his apostolic example. We are called upon to do the same according to the human needs of our day. The deeper our union with Christ, the more we feel the weight of this responsibility. Pope Paul VI, in an apostolic letter on social justice, mentions the obligation we have not only to work for the heavenly kingdom to come, but also for the betterment of all in this earthly kingdom. He said: "Animated by the power of the Spirit of Jesus Christ, the Savior of mankind, and upheld by hope, the Christian involves himself in the building up of the human city, one that is to be peaceful, just, fraternal, and acceptable as an offering to God. In fact, the expectation of a new earth must not weaken but rather stimulate our concern for cultivating this one..."

You, perhaps, have heard of Archbishop Helder Camara of Recife, Brazil, in South America. He had put himself on the line for human justice. In 1974, he was awarded the People's Peace Prize, the alternative to the Nobel Peace Prize. When he received the St. Francis Peace Medal a few years ago, he made this statement: "Poor Man of Assisi, Minstrel of Lady Poverty! What would you do in a world in which two-thirds of the population have far exceeded the limits of poverty, and have fallen into misery... You had, and you still have, the greatest respect for Lady Poverty, but it seems to me that, without a doubt, you would never call misery a lady."

The archbishop really believes that if St. Francis were alive today, he would speak to the super rich and the oppressors of those in misery about Lady Justice. He feels that the Poor Man of Assisi would denounce injustice on all levels and opt for the oppressed. Should we not give serious consideration to acting in Francis' name today and speak and act in the name of Lady Justice? Does not this article of the rule call for this? Just read these words of the archbishop: "Come Lord. Do not smile and say you are already with us. Millions do not know you, and to us who do, what is the difference? What is the point of your presence if our lives do not alter? Change our lives, shatter our complacency. Make your word flesh of our flesh, blood of our blood, and our live's purpose. Take away the quietness of a clear conscience. Press us uncomfortably. For only this that other peace is made, your peace."

We can all embrace a simpler form of life and avoid consuming too much food and energy. Yet this is not enough. A more modest life style can be a powerful witness in the struggle against hunger, and we may be able to share more of our funds with others. But it really needs to be accompanied with our efforts to change public policy. Giving up some food can easily give us a false sense of fulfillment. When we hold off in buying a new or used car, a heater or air-conditioner, and the like, we are truly fighting consumerism. But unless such actions are accompanied by more positive steps, we may do nothing more than put some men or women out of work.

There is a need to have more vision. We must realize that more people require a greater share of the per capita United States growth. As a result, the most vital sacrifice we can make is the sacrifice of our time and energy to change public policy. Letters to the members of the United States Congress must be written in order to influence them in the proper direction. These letters do make a difference. This has been proven. So we must beware of our laziness or procrastination. We can be informed of the justice issues at stake by such monthly publications as the newsletter of Bread for the World and your diocesan newspaper. All this takes a little work. But what about work?

PROPER ATTITUDE TOWARDS WORK

Article 16 of the rule recommends wisely that "we esteem work as a gift and as a sharing in the creation, redemption, and service of the human community." St. Francis always spoke about "the grace of working." Some people seem never to have adequately possessed this grace or they lost it. It is an important grace, and we should always be happy and grateful if we have it.

There always is a tension between Martha and Mary, between work and prayer. There is no easy solution to this tension. It is rather something which we must strive to bring into harmony or proper balance. It is not necessary to allow our work to be a distraction from our life of prayer or a burden that we must endure.

We must learn to grow through prayer and reflection into a greater consciousness of Christ and do our work in union with him. St. Paul wrote that whatever we do, whether we eat or drink, all should be done for the greater honor and glory of God. St. Francis also had as his motto, "My God and My All" and this "my all" included his work. His work was creative, healing, and a true service to others.

The notion of being sent into the world with Christ to work is a constant theme of the Gospel. St. John, for instance, brings this out at the beginning of the Last Supper narrative. Jesus tells his disciples: "He who accepts anyone I send accepts me, and in accepting me accepts him who sent me" (Jn 13:20). The idea that the Father's sending of the son is continued in the Son's sending of his disciples is repeated even more forcefully in the resurrection narrative: "As the Father has sent me, so I send you" (Jn 20:21). We, as apostles, are called to share in the life of the Trinity precisely by joining the Son in his mission to this suffering and broken world. "I made known to you all that I heard from my Father. It was not you who chose me, it was I who chose you to go forth and bear fruit" (Jn 15:15-16).

Christ spent more time at work, on the road for the Father, than he did in formal prayer. In healing the sick, raising the dead, teaching in the temple or on the wayside, or proclaiming unpopular values to pharisees and others, Jesus reveals the price he had to pay in carrying out the mission entrusted to him by his Father. It was only on occasion that he could withdraw to a desert place or a hidden spot for prayer. This dusty, sweaty mission of Christ is the model of our daily work.

chapter eleven

Enriching Our Family Life

T *17. In their family, they should cultivate the Franciscan spirit of peace, fidelity, and respect for life, striving to make of it a sign of a world already renewed in Christ.*

By living the grace of matrimony, husbands and wives, in particular, should bear witness in the world to the love of Christ for his Church. They should joyfully accompany their children on their human and spiritual journey by providing a simple and open Christian education and being attentive to the vocation of each child.

Article 17 of the Rule of the Secular Franciscan Order urges all members to enrich their families with the Franciscan spirit. Husbands and wives, by living in the grace of sacramental marriage, express to the world the love of Christ for his Church; and their efforts in behalf of the spiritual, moral, and physical lives of their children will challenge them to follow in the sacrificial footsteps of Christ.

WHOLESOME FAMILY LIFE

A man and a woman living together, fully aware of their sacramental union in Christ, are a tremendous force for good. When love is deep and sacrificial between them, it spills over to their children and all who know them. It is in such a family that deep interpersonal relationships are formed and are lived out. These are the foundations for the stability of most peoples' lives and, therefore, of society itself. A stable relationship of husband and wife is characterized by mutual respect, intimacy, fidelity, communication, trust, and understanding. These are virtues all husbands and wives must seek continually: they do not just happen but require mutual prayer and sacrifice.

When parents are striving to inculcate these virtues in themselves, they create a healthy atmosphere for their children. Then it is possible for children to know themselves as individuals and in relation to other persons. In a good family, children should gradually be able to crystallize their own sexualities, form basic values of good citizenship, and achieve normal satisfaction, confidence, and security besides coming to God as a loving Father.

A happy family also cushions the shocks of life and eases the pains that come to everyone. In the family circle, every member should be loved not for what they do or make but simply because they are. Here, too, all the members acquire a sense of continuity with the past and a sense of commitment to the future.

It is all too clear that parents cannot perform their duties alone. They can easily be overwhelmed by forces which they cannot influence or control. To help them, we must address ourselves less to the criticism and reform of parents themselves than to the criticism and reform of the institutions that sap their self-esteem and power. All of us must attempt to make available to parents the help they need to give them enough power so they can be effective advocates with and coordinators of the other forces that are bringing up their children. We must all work to promote economic and social growth in the context of family relationships and not only for individual persons.

As Archbishop Gerety of Newark, New Jersey, had said: "What we need now is a rebirth of nerve based in Christian hope, a new commitment rooted in faith to the perduring values of marriage and family life, a renewed confidence in the power of God's grace given through the sacramental bond of marriage." Hence, good parents must be ready to risk as they perform their duties and believe that God will see them to a blessed conclusion.

Pope Paul VI, in his apostolic exhortation on "Evangelization in the Modern World," said that the family should carry on spiritual ministry. He wrote: "One cannot fail to stress the evangelizing apostolate of the family in the evangelizing apostolate of the laity. At different moments in the Church's history and also in the Second Vatican Council, the family has well deserved the beautiful title of the domestic church. This means that there should be found in every Christian family the various aspects of the entire Church... In a family which is conscious of this mission, all members evangelize and are evangelized... And such a family becomes the evangelizer of many other families and of the neighborhood of which it forms a part."

The great love of Christ and St. Francis should pervade every family. Secular Franciscans have been called to follow the Gospel. The Gospel has rightly been called love in action. It is a love that forgives, that continues on despite ingratitude, that remains faithful in the face of the weakness of a husband, wife, or child. In a word, it is a love that is not afraid of self-sacrifice. Such a love is a true evangelizing force both within and without the family.

A CHALLENGE TO PARENTS

It is no easy task today for parents to pass on their Catholic spiritual values to their children. Formerly, it was enough to be born of Catholic parents, learn prayers within the family, listen to religious stories from the Bible, receive instruction and sacramental preparation in parish schools or confraternity classes, worship regularly, and receive the sacraments. This method was not foolproof; but it worked with remarkable frequency. Today, this religious culture often no longer has these good effects. Parents cannot depend upon these practices to truly help all of their children preserve their faith.

Besides this, the surrounding culture of society no longer supports church attendance. Religious identity can no longer be kept alive only by religious family customs and practices. Sterner stuff is necessary, namely, personal conviction and free choice.

Often, one or both parents, as well as children, have almost a total lack of authentic religious experience, particularly an absence of meaningful personal prayer and a missing sense of the sacred. We naturally hope Secular Franciscan parents do possess these, at least in some degree. But there is also the ailment of constriction of the heart or a narrowness of the horizons.

So many teenagers who want to be "good persons" believe they can do this alone and unaided. Hence, God is unnecessary and the Church is a nuisance. What they need, in order to change this attitude, is not religious information but an expansion of their heart's desires, so that they may ask the questions Christ came to answer and long for the things he came to give. In a word, they must be open to the transcendent, hungry for the fullness of life.

For the older teenager, the way to such questioning and seeking is best found through human relationships. They are looking for friendship and understanding. Hence, they are not seeking a God who is an authority figure but a God of love and understanding. This is the type of God revealed by Jesus Christ. He is not a miracle or a superman, but a loving person who asks for integrity in relationships, for maturity that is possible only to those who are truly open to others.

But even more remains to be done than to establish this relationship. As they are invited to take this second look at their religious tradition, they must be able to see it whole before they see it in detail. Parents must inform them that the faith community that has nurtured them thus far and now invites them to free, adult membership, is more than a group of good people who share wholesome ideals. They must understand that we are more than a movement. That we are a Church sharing a faith that makes demands beyond the ordinary and offering the assurance of a life stronger than death. More, that we are an organism, the very Body of Christ, with the Holy Spirit as its vital principle.

Then, we must indicate that we have the sacraments to back up our human efforts to live up to Christ's values to which we are committed. And among these, we particularly have the Eucharist as our food. Yet parents and teenagers must remember there should be nothing like "cheap grace" as Dietrich Bonhoeffer, in his book *Cost of Discipleship* points out. Cheap grace is grace without discipleship, grace without the cross, grace without Jesus Christ, living and incarnate. No one should partake of Christ's gifts without concern for Christ the giver. Otherwise, the recipient runs the great risk of receiving no grace. Too many children are baptized and walked through the rest of the sacraments without a faith-sharing family or community around them. They run the risk of becoming baptized unbelievers. We can best remedy this by working and praying to make our families and the families we associate with faith communities. This is what our Secular Franciscanism is all about if it is genuine. Young people must be able to see a quality of adult faith that they can recognize and respect. Therefore, parents must evangelize themselves first.

chapter twelve

Universal Kinship

T *18. Moreover, they should respect all creatures, animate and inanimate, which "bear the imprint of the Most High," and they should strive to move from the temptation of exploiting creation to the Franciscan concept of universal kinship.*

A respect for all creatures, animate and inanimate, and avoiding the exploitation of creation are treated in the 18th Article of the rule because these are traits that found telling expression in the life of St. Francis. Our happiness is also, in a great measure, dependent on the quality of the world in which we life.

ST. FRANCIS AND CREATION

Perhaps, St. Francis' tremendous appreciation of God's created world, and all in it, is the strongest impression most people have of him. They respect or love him because of his gentle and warm treatment extended to all persons, animals, inanimate objects, in a word, everything made by God. The world was the work of God, and it always reminded him of God and his almighty power. As a result, he had a profound appreciation of his environment. He was so careful not to be a mere user of creatures and created things. He was more. He was a careful and thoughtful steward of them.

Francis was well aware that he was part of creation and was not a rugged individualist who walked through life foolishly using things and tossing them about wantonly. Humbly, Francis regarded himself only a peer with all the rest of creation. From this viewpoint, he could call all creatures his brothers and sisters, and God was the Father of many different sons and daughters.

As the English-speaking Franciscan provincial ministers wrote in the booklet *St. Francis and the New Materialism:* "Francis had a powerful sense of rightness about humanity's relationship to its environment. He understood that because it came from God, because it constituted a family of sons and daughters, because humanity depends so much upon it, it must always be treated respectfully, even though difficult, hostile, and dangerous. We know from our dealings with people that to respect another—even when he or she is an enemy—is a summons to peace and reconciliation. Francis, therefore, calls us to live not at odds with nature as with reluctant prey, but to live in harmony with it, full of respect and care."

Thoroughly conscious of being a child of God, Francis considered all his fellow creatures to be his kin, as members of the one, great family of God. In all of them, he was thrilled at the wisdom, power, and goodness of the Creator. As he viewed the sun, the moon, water, creatures large or small, he was filled with joy and reverence. They were all, in a sense, sacred and deserved to be treated as such. He built a bond of delightful harmony around the world which was reminiscent of the peace which existed between man and nature at the dawn of creation. As Father Hilarin Felder, OFMCap wrote: "His love-call resounded throughout the entire sense-world and was echoed back to him in loving esteem and obedience of all nature." Francis could not misuse creatures or created objects because they spoke to him of God. All creation kept saying to him, "Lift up your heart and praise the Lord." As the Three Young Men in the fiery furnace in the Old Testament called upon the elements of the universe to praise and honor the Father of all things, so, too, Francis never tired of praising and blessing the Author and Preserver in all the elements and in every living thing.

Francis suffered on seeing created things mistreated. He would not let a brother throw burning or smoking wood outside, as it was commonly done, but had it spread carefully on the ground out of reverence for God of whom the fire is a creature. He also told his brothers who cut firewood not to chop down whole trees, but to cut only a part of a tree so as to leave a part standing. Many more incidents could be cited. They all go to show his great respect for nature in all its forms and how he detested any exploitation of nature.

WE AND CREATION

To be really Franciscan, we must also have a great respect for the created world and avoid any exploitation of it. This is all the more important in our day when the world is already suffering from environmental deterioration and depletion of its resources.

We must keep ourselves from the wild spirit of materialism and also help others to overcome it. As Fr. Thomas Dubay stated: "If adaptation to the modern world has actually meant settling for a more comfortable life, a rejection of the hard road and the narrow gate, it is no renewal at all. If updating in a religious congregation has consisted largely of mitigations, we have a clear sign of resistance to the Spirit of the Living God. If the renewal of moral theology consistently means more pleasure and less sacrifice, it is no updating at all. It is a surrender to the world."

Our Rule of the Secular Franciscans is a renewed and deeper call to the gospel ideals. It demands sacrifice on our part and a checking of our carelessness in using created things. With the decrease in our earth's non-renewable resources (oil, natural gas, iron, zinc, etc.), a change is demanded in our consumeristic practices. When we likewise consume more than our rightful share, we are selfish and lacking in the gospel spirit. Genuine conversion is demonstrated by the individual who, having two tunics, gives one to his brother or sister who has none (Lk 3:10-11).

It behooves each of us as individuals and as fraternity to consider our attitude and relationship when we maintain with the created world. How far are we from the spirit and practice of St. Francis? We must bring ourselves to the practical realization that we have a grave responsibility as followers of Christ and Francis toward our environment and our resources. This calls for prayer and careful consideration of God, our fellow persons, and all created things.

Then, we all need to become more informed about our resources and understand the interdependence of all people throughout the reverence for God of whom the fire is a creature. He also told his brothers who cut firewood not to chop down whole trees, but to cut only a part of a tree so as to leave a part standing. Many more incidents could be cited. They all go to show his great respect for nature in all its forms and how he detested any exploitation of nature.

WE AND CREATION

To be really Franciscan, we must also have a great respect for the created world and avoid any exploitation of it. This is all the more important in our day when the world is already suffering from environmental deterioration and depletion of its resources.

We must keep ourselves from the wild spirit of materialism and also help others to overcome it. As Fr. Thomas Dubay stated: "If adaptation to the modern world has actually meant settling for a more comfortable life, a rejection of the hard road and the narrow gate, it is no renewal at all. If updating in a religious congregation has consisted largely of mitigations, we have a clear sign of resistance to the Spirit of the Living God. If the renewal of moral theology consistently means more pleasure and less sacrifice, it is no updating at all. It is a surrender to the world."

Our Rule of the Secular Franciscans is a renewed and deeper call to the gospel ideals. It demands sacrifice on our part and a checking of our carelessness in using created things. With the decrease in our earth's non-renewable resources (oil, natural gas, iron, zinc, etc.), a change is demanded in our consumeristic practices. When we likewise consume more than our rightful share, we are selfish and lacking in the gospel spirit. Genuine conversion is demonstrated by the individual who, having two tunics, gives one to his brother or sister who has none (Lk 3:10-11).

It behooves each of us as individuals and as fraternity to consider our attitude and relationship when we maintain with the created world. How far are we from the spirit and practice of St. Francis? We must bring ourselves to the practical realization that we have a grave responsibility as followers of Christ and Francis toward our environment and our resources. This calls for prayer and careful consideration of God, our fellow persons, and all created things.

Then, we all need to become more informed about our resources and understand the interdependence of all people throughout the

chapter thirteen

Our Call to Peace

T 19. Mindful that they are bearers of peace which must be built up unceasingly, they should seek out ways of unity and fraternal harmony through dialogue, trusting in the presence of the divine seed in everyone and in the transforming power of love and pardon.

Messengers of perfect joy in every circumstance, they should strive to bring joy and hope to others.

Since they are immersed in the resurrection of Christ, which gives true meaning to Sister Death, let them serenely tend toward the ultimate encounter with the Father.

A desire and a love for peace are tied deeply into the lives of every human being. Yet true peace is illusive. St. Francis in the spirit of the Gospel was a great exponent of Christian peace. The 19th Article of the rule for Secular Franciscans takes note of this and declares that all of the members should strive to be instruments of peace.

PEACE: A FRANCISCAN CHARACTERISTIC

Christ's words "Peace be with you" had a significant effect on St. Francis. He reflected deeply on Christ's gospel teaching about peace, and he made it his own. How did Francis prepare himself to be a man of peace? Fr. Isidore O'Brien, in his life of Francis of Assisi, gives us a very good reply to this question. He wrote: "He who lived so completely by the Gospel realized with a clarity grasped by few the evangelical truth that penance, sincere and strong, must precede peace, as the needle must precede the thread. Does not the Gospel itself, the Christ-given charter of peace, begin with John's cry to those who had come to the wilderness to hear him: 'Repent, for the kingdom of heaven is a hand'? (Mt 3:2). That is, Christ was about to come forth and preach to all that the way to salvation lies along the hard road of penance. 'Jesus came into Galilee preaching: Repent and believe in the Gospel'" (Mk 1:15).

Francis experienced this conversion himself. He recognized that an individual change of heart was necessary to truly embrace the gospel way of life, the road to peace. Hence, he preached penance or a change of heart. Perhaps, the biggest and the main effect of his preaching brought about the formation of the Order of Penitents, as the Secular Franciscan Order was first known. This Secular Franciscan Order was the instrument of peace to individuals and entire communities. From the very beginning, Secular Franciscans were forbidden to bear arms; and this helped, in a large measure, to destroy feudalism along with its petty wars. The feudal lords had to look far and long to find any soldiers. So they could not carry on their unjust wars. When Cardinal Hugolino, St. Francis' friend, became Pope Gregory IX, he permitted Secular Franciscans to take oaths as peacemakers, in defense of the faith, in self-defense and as witnesses in court. It is well to keep in mind that the oath not to carry arms applied only to unjust wars.

Francis himself, during the Crusades, had walked calmly through enemy lines to confront the Sultan, the enemy of the Christians. He profoundly affected the Sultan though he did not convert him. But the Sultan gave him safe conduct back to his homeland.

Perhaps, St. Francis' entire spirit as a man of peace is seen most vividly in his encounter with the vicious wolf of Gubbio. The legend is well known. St. Francis confronted the fearful wolf and brought about a change of heart. The wolf became a friend of the villagers who fed him. Francis, like the early Secular Franciscans, spread this brotherly spirit among the townsfolk and their former enemy.

When Francis heard the words of Christ as he commissioned his apostles for active duty, "As you go into a house say, Peace be with you," he considered these words, as well as his vocation, as a direct revelation to himself. All his life, he held to the reality of this revelation; and even at the very close of his life, he stated: "The Lord revealed to me this salutation, that we should say: The Lord give you peace."

At the time the local bishop and the governor were involved in a serious dispute, and the bishop had excommunicated the governor while the governor ordered that no one sell anything to the bishop, Francis was moved to great pity. He made every effort and succeeded in restoring peace between them. It was at this time he also added another verse to his Canticle of the Sun, and it was on peace. It reads: "Praised be my Lord for those who for your love forgive, and weakness bear and tribulation. Blessed those who shall in peace endure, for by you, Most High, shall they be crowned."

St. Francis also openly espoused the cause of the lower classes because of the disadvantages they suffered. As a result, he selected for himself and his followers the title of "Minores," Friars Minor. But he always sought peace between all classes. The Franciscan conception of poverty and humility, of universal brotherhood, was in itself, as Fr. Hilarin Felder, OFMCap wrote, a powerful factor in promoting the cause of the people; indeed, it has been said very appropriately, that the Franciscan Rule was the consecration, in a manner the cradle, of democracy, especially in Italy.

It was the determination of St. Francis always to share in the blessing of the Beatitude: "Blessed are the peacemakers, for they shall be called the children of God."

OUR SHARE IN SOWING PEACE

Article 19 of the rule directs all Secular Franciscans "that they are bearers of peace which must be built up unceasingly, they should seek out ways of unity and fraternal harmony through dialogue, trusting in the presence of the divine seed in everyone and in the transforming power of love and pardon." God did implant "the divine seed in everyone," namely, the God-given desire to live in peace and bring peace to others. It is this seed that we must cultivate in ourselves and others. The stronger it grows, the hardier the peace will be.

The transforming power of love and pardon is very formidable.

When we, for the love of God and others, talk ourselves out of anger, resentment, and revenge, we open ourselves and others to peace. A spirit of calm comes like a soft and soothing balm into our lives.

A renowned example of a person of peace today is Mother Teresa of Calcutta, India. When the Nobel Prize was presented to her, John Sanness, the chairman of the Norwegian Nobel Committee, gave this explanation of the choice of Mother Teresa for the award. "The year 1979 has not been a year of peace: disputes and conflicts between nations, peoples and ideologies have been conducted with all the accompanying extremes of inhumanity and cruelty. We are faced with a new and overwhelming flood of refugees; not without reason, the word genocide has been on many lips. Because of this, the committee considered it right and appropriate to choose Mother Teresa. The committee posed a focal question: can any political, social or intellectual feat of engineering on the international or national plane, no matter how effective and rational... give us anything but a house built on sand, unless the spirit of Mother Teresa inspires the builders."

Mother Teresa has summed up her spirit in these words: "I believe in person to person; every person is Christ for me, and since there is only one Jesus, that person is the only person in the world for me at that time." How true this is to the spirit of St. Francis. How true our spirit should be to it. It is the key to the possibility of all of us being peacemakers in our every day lives.

The popular Peace Prayer of St. Francis adequately expresses the saint's spirit and is a well-tailored program for all of us to live by. "Lord make me an instrument of your peace," is a powerful petition in itself if we truly wish him to make us this instrument. Our dispositions and gospel attitude are prerequisites before God can ever give us the grace to be such an instrument.

It is well for all of us to pray this Prayer of Peace each day and reflect upon it. It is a loaded prayer. In it, we are asking God to make us an apostle of love, pardon, faith, hope, light, and joy. It is asking to shoulder a great deal. Perhaps, more than we are ready for, unless we prepare ourselves with a grounding in humility and service.

Christ is known as the suffering servant. Francis endeavored to emulate his role. We, too, must strive to be suffering servants. It requires a good deal of reflection on the life of Christ and an openness to grace. As we grow in being a suffering servant, the Peace

Prayer of St. Francis will be ever more meaningful to us and aid us in becoming real apostles of peace.

Pax et Bonum, Peace and every Good, is the distinctive Franciscan motto. It is a phrase given to us by St. Francis, and it has been kept very much alive through its faithful use by his followers. We are to go about expressing peace and goodness and thus sow the seeds of it everywhere. This phrase, "Pax et Bonum," is really to be uttered as a blessing to others, because peace and every good thing are great blessings from which joy flows.

In this way, as the 19th Article of the rule indicates, we will bring joy and hope to others. When we have peace, we can rejoice together in the Lord. St. Francis had no patience with gloom. He was anxious that his followers show themselves as joyful in the Lord.

Fr. Lazaro Iriarte de Aspurz, OFMCap had this to say about joy: "Joy is found in the meeting of things of the senses with things of the spirit. Happiness, to which man aspires with his whole being, is attained when he enters into the joy of the Lord. St. Francis prayed, 'You are peace. You are joy and gladness.' And that eternal, inexhaustible joy of divine plentitude is what Christ has come to communicate to men. Jesus reacted openly against the pharisaical gloomy look and a long face; his manner of honoring with a smile wanted his followers to be joyful and attractive even when they fasted." This is the joy that St. Francis understood, practiced, and desired his followers to seek and possess.

Joy is a powerful ingredient that can mean a great deal for us as we think of the resurrection of Christ, prepare for Sister Death, and hurry on our way to our Heavenly Father.

chapter fourteen

A Brotherhood Movement

T 20. *The Secular Franciscan Order is divided into fraternities of various levels—local, regional, national, and international. Each one has its own moral personality in the Church. These various fraternities are coordinated and united according to the norm of this rule and of the constitutions.*

21. On various levels, each fraternity is animated and guided by a council and minister (or president) who are elected by the professed according to the constitutions.

Their service, which lasts for a definite period, is marked by a ready and willing spirit and is a duty of responsibility to each member and to the community.

Within themselves the fraternities are structured in different ways according to the norm of the constitutions, according to the various needs of their members and their regions, and under the guidance of their respective council.

22. The local fraternity is to be established canonically. It becomes the basic unit of the whole Order and a visible sign of the Church, the community of love. This should be the privileged place for developing a sense of Church and the Franciscan vocation and for enlivening the apostolic life of its members.

The third chapter of the rule, as in the former rule, covers the government of the Franciscan Secular Order. Its three opening articles are declarations on the self-government of the Order by its respective fraternity councils.

A CALL TO RESPONSIBILITY

The Secular Franciscan Order is not structured as a corporation or institution, but as a brotherhood. This is accomplished by the establishment of fraternities at various levels: local, regional, national, and international. Most Secular Franciscans think of fraternity only on the local level. But the rule calls upon the members to have a broader outlook. The whole Secular Franciscan Order is called a fraternity, an international one, since it embraces all of the members throughout the world. The national fraternity includes all of those in a certain country; the regional fraternity, those in a given geographic area within a province; and the local fraternity, those in a particular neighborhood.

As the rule states, each one of these fraternities has its own moral personality in the Church. What is meant by the phrase "its own moral personality"? "Moral person" is a canonical term (used in Church law) that refers to a juridical person rather than a human being. Thus a parish, certain pious associations, religious orders, seminaries, and the like, are constituted as moral persons. A moral person, by its very nature, is perpetual; but it can be legitimately suppressed. Hence, when we say that a fraternity has its own moral personality, we mean that once established by legitimate authority, it has a right to exist and function according to its purpose.

It is mentioned in the rule that the various fraternities are coordinated and united according to the norm of this rule and of the constitutions. *[Editorial Note: The Secular Franciscan Order has a new International General Constitution which was approved in the year 1990 by the Holy See, after the revision of Canon Law. The Secular Franciscans around the world are going through the experience of living by these constitutions which will be finalized and formalized in 1999.]*

A very important and innovative feature of article 21 of the rule is that it established the Secular Franciscan Order in its own right as a mature member of the Franciscan family in much the same way as the Fist and Second Orders of St. Francis. It is an equal member of the Franciscan family, affiliated to the First Order and Third Order Regular only for spiritual assistance and inspiration. Formerly, there was a real dependency on the part of the Secular Franciscan Order on the First Order and the Third Order Regular. The Secular Franciscans now have the direct responsibility for their own Order and its general welfare.

The Second Vatican Council declared laypersons to be mature Catholics and that they should be prepared to make responsible decisions in the light of the principles of the Church. The Rule of the Secular Franciscan Order is merely implementing the directives of Vatican II. In regard to the laity, Vatican II, in the document on the Dogmatic Constitution of the Church, states: "The laity are gathered together in the People of God and make up the Body of Christ under one Head. Whoever they are, they are called upon, as living members, to expend all their energy for the growth of the Church and its continuous sanctification. For this very energy is a gift of the Creator and a blessing of the Redeemer... Each individual layman must stand before the world as a witness to the resurrection and life of the Lord Jesus and as a sign that God lives. As a body and individually, the laity must do their part to nourish the world with spiritual fruits, and to spread abroad in it that spirit by which are animated those poor, meek, and peacemaking men whom the Lord in the Gospel calls blessed. In a word, what the soul is to the body, let Christians be to the world."

FUNCTIONING OF THE FRATERNITIES

In accord with the Franciscan democratic spirit, the rule declares that "each fraternity is animated and guided by a council and minister (or president) who are elected by the professed according to the constitutions." They serve in office for a definite period.

The president and the other officers of the council on all levels are called to a ministry of service, which as the rule states "is marked by a ready and willing spirit and is a duty of responsibility to each member and to the community." A true fraternity leader performs the threefold function of Christ: namely, his priestly, prophetic, and kingly offices as outlined in the Vatican Document for the laity.

The priestly function calls upon the officers to offer up all their works to God that they may be acceptable to him. In this way, they consecrate the world itself to God as they carry out their duties.

As to the prophetic function, the officers witness openly to their faith in Christ, speaking cheerfully and bravely about this faith as it pertains to the ordinary things of life. They constantly strive to understand the revealed truths better and assist others to do the same.

The kingly function of the officers demands that they work to conquer sin in themselves by true penance and an openness to grace, while at the same time reaching out to others in a Christ-like service. They are to be particularly concerned with the sick and shut-in members.

Good fraternity leaders do not do everything themselves, but obtain the cooperation of others and develop leadership in them as well. In this way, they create a healthy community spirit which is so vital to all of the members and the fraternity itself.

As has always been the practice, each fraternity must be canonically erected. This means it must have the consent of the local Bishop and the acceptance of the Provincial Minister of the Friar Province to which it would then be affiliated.

Fraternities need not be cast in the same mold. The rule allows for diversity from one fraternity to another. Local needs and circumstances may warrant a special structure or mode of functioning for a fraternity. This is certainly beneficial for the well being of the entire Secular Franciscan Order as well as the individual fraternity. With this elasticity, various fraternities can achieve definite objectives more easily and effectively. Since the local fraternity is the basic unit of the whole Order, it is a visible sign of the Church when it functions according to the spirit of Christ and Francis. A good fraternity is a privileged community in which the members can develop a sense of the Church, the Franciscan vocation, and the apostolic lives of its members.

chapter fifteen

Entering the Secular Franciscan Order

T *23. Requests for admission to the Secular Franciscan Order must be presented to the local fraternity whose council decides upon the acceptance of new brothers and sisters.*

Admission into the Order is gradually attained through a time of initiation, a period of formation of at least one year, and profession of the rule. The entire community is engaged in this process of growth by its own manner of living. The age for profession and the distinctive Franciscan sign are regulated by the statues.

Profession by its nature is a permanent commitment.

Members who find themselves in particular difficulties should discuss their problems with the council in fraternal dialogue. Withdrawal or permanent dismissal from the Order, if necessary, is an act of the fraternity council according to the norm of the constitutions.

Article 23 of the Secular Franciscan Rule covers the vital material on admission, formation and profession. Its purpose is to introduce a prospective member in an orderly way to the gospel life as seen and lived by St. Francis.

ADMISSION OF MEMBERS

People are drawn to the Franciscan way of life in varying ways. Some are inspired by active members; others are advised by their confessors; others are animated by reading and studying the life of St. Francis; others are propelled by their search for a practical manner of living the Gospel; others have a family tradition of desiring to be Franciscan in their life style. The enumeration could go on, giving us a patch-quilt path to the Secular Franciscan Order. Behind all, however, is the individual person's response to God's calling to a deeper union and dedication to Christ.

Christ does not impose his will on anyone. He invites all to accept the complete good news of the Gospel as we see it incarnated in him. This is precisely what happened to St. Francis one year when he heard the Gospel of St. Matthew (10:7-20) read. He explained: "That's what I want! That is what I am looking for! With my whole heart I long to do that!"

This call of Christ given to a prospective member must be approved by the proper authority. The proper authority in the case of the Secular Franciscan Order is the local fraternity council, the local officers. Their approval is necessary for anyone to be admitted into the Order. A fraternity council is to pray and use prudent judgment in admitting members. A candidate should be flexible, open to grace, sound in faith, ready to serve God and others, and anxious to grow in ever deeper union with God.

Today, the acceptable age for membership is usually 18 years or not too old as to be set in one's ways and closed to Franciscan formation. The practice of having new members spend at least six months in a period of inquiry is certainly a wise means of preparation. During these six months, a new member is given a general idea of the Secular Franciscan Order, the life of St. Francis, and the customs and regulations of the local fraternity being joined.

The admission or reception ceremony is relatively simple. The full celebration takes place at the time of profession. But the admission ceremony is important since it marks the break with worldly attitudes and an embracing of the new life of the Gospel. Here, the change of heart begins that is to bloom and blossom in a Christlike way the rest of one's life. This is symbolized by the ritual words casting aside the old self and old works and putting on the new person Christ. The signs or symbols of a cord and scapular or a properly designated medal are used in the investiture ceremony to emphasize this along with the presentation to the new member of the copy of the Franciscan Gospel Rule of Life.

Formerly, it was always the practice to give the new member a new name, a Franciscan patron, to emphasize the new way of life. Now it is optional but still a very effective manner of impressing on the new member that a new life is being started, a Franciscan way of living. This practice of taking a new name originated from the Bible. There, we see God giving new names to those he calls to a special vocation. For example, you recall that Abram's name was changed to Abraham, Jacob's to Israel, Simon's to Peter.

FRANCISCAN GOSPEL FORMATION

The introduction into the Franciscan gospel way of life carries with it a year of formation. This is necessary for a proper grasp and understanding of St. Francis' ideals and principles along with the directives peculiar to the Secular Franciscan Order. The formation can take various forms. There are numerous texts that can be used, but the instruction should be given at least once a month for the period of a year. It should naturally be supplemented by the reading of some Franciscan-oriented magazine or periodical and informative Franciscan books.

Prayer, of course, is very essential during the year of formation. The light and guidance of the Holy Spirit are needed. The continuing growth of the metanoia or change of heart will never be accomplished without the Holy Spirit. Every member's Franciscan life must be the result of unreserved and cheerful acceptance of the operation of the Lord in them and a ready cooperation with grace.

A very strong factor in the formation of new members is the action of the entire fraternal community. No one can be formed in a vacuum. We all know the formative atmosphere created for children in a good family rooted in faith and common sense. Hence, when a fraternity has a sound Franciscan spirit and lives it, new members receive their best formation. Example speaks louder than words and lasts much longer. A healthy Franciscan fraternity in which the members practice the Franciscan way of life will produce the best members. Here, the words of any formation text are speaking and living in daily experience and make the text itself of far less importance. In such a case, all of the members of the fraternity participate effectively with the formation director in forming new members.

PROFESSION OR COMMITMENT

The year of formation or time of candidacy culminates in the new member making profession. Again, it is the officers of the fraternity that declare a member is ready for profession. Usually, the time of candidacy is a period of one year; but it can be extended by the council where this is deemed prudent.

Where possible, profession takes place during the Sacrifice of Holy Mass after the spiritual assistant's homily or conference. This ceremony has a more solemn character than the reception. The main symbol of the profession ceremony is the crucifix which is presented to each newly-professed member. It is known as the profession crucifix. It represents the fact that the professed member embraces the whole Christ, the suffering servant.

The crucifix also emphasizes the permanency of the profession. Christ embraced the cross, was nailed to it, and remained firm to the very end. The Secular Franciscan Rule envisions that once profession is made by a member, it is permanent: until death. This is what real gospel life means: "No one, having put his hand to the plough and looking back is fit for the kingdom of heaven."

God knows that we are weak. But our weakness is his opportunity. We may stumble along, but God will lift us up in our weakness as long as we lean on him in faith, hope, and love. In our era, many fear to make a permanent commitment because of their flabby faith, hope and love of God. They are afraid to risk due to their preoccupation with themselves. Ever on the alert for self-fulfillment, they fail to grasp that Christ has not promised self-fulfillment. He has rather stated: "If you wish to be my disciple, deny your very self, take up your cross and come after me."

Happiness that is genuine comes to us only when we have made a permanent commitment. Despite the changing times, the great progress in scientific and technological circles, and the development of theological knowledge, a permanent commitment is the best goal for anyone. We are not created to hang loose in society but to take firm and definite strides forward. A permanent commitment to the Franciscan life allows you ample room to adjust in our present changing. The Holy Spirit is always there to guide and inspire.

Secular Franciscans who persevere in their commitments have every right to celebrate special jubilees along the way, as their 25th, 50th, or 60th year as Franciscans. Such celebrations are an inspiration to all members and contribute a great deal to the firmer belief of all the members in the permanency of their commitments.

chapter sixteen

Fraternal
Responsibilities

T 24. To foster communion among members, the council should organize regular and frequent meetings of the community as well as meeting with other Franciscan groups, especially with youth groups. It should adopt appropriate means for growth in Franciscan and ecclesial life and encourage everyone to a life of fraternity. This communion continues with deceased brothers and sisters through prayer for them

25. Regarding expenses necessary for the life of the fraternity and the needs of worship, of the apostolate and of charity, all the brothers and sisters should offer a contribution according to their means. Local fraternities should contribute toward the expenses of the higher fraternity councils.

26. As a concrete sign of communion and coresponsibility, the councils on various levels, in keeping with the constitutions, shall ask for suitable and well prepared religious for spiritual assistance. They should make this request to the superiors of the four religious Franciscan families, to whom the Secular Fraternity has been united for centuries.

To promote fidelity to the charism as well as observance of the *rule and to receive greater support in the life of the fraternity, the minister or president, with the consent of the council, should take care to ask for a regular pastoral visit by the competent religious superior as well as for a fraternity visit from those of the higher fraternities, according to the norm of the constitutions.*

"And whoever shall keep these words, may he or she be filled in heaven with the blessing of the Most High Father, and on earth with the blessing of His beloved Son, together with that of the Most Holy Spirit, the Paraclete..." (Blessing of St. Francis in the Testament)

The last three articles of the Rule of the Secular Franciscan Order cover vital matters about meetings, the common fund, spiritual direction, and official visitation of the fraternities.

VARIOUS MEETINGS OF MEMBERS

Communication among Secular Franciscans is fostered on a local level principally through the fraternity meetings. A fraternity usually expects its members to participate in a monthly meeting. This is a very necessary gathering of the members for their continued formation and for communicating the goals and programs of a province, a region, and the fraternity itself.

A hospitality committee appointed by the local fraternity council can do a great deal to help members feel at home and become acquainted with each other. An identification badge for each member is an added means of inviting members to know each other. Many can remember faces but forget names, and people appreciate being called by their proper names. It is a real act of charity to wear an identification badge to declare your openness to your fellow members and help them to know you.

Many fraternities have one or two extra smaller specialized meetings each month for the benefit of their members. These can be either a discussion meeting, a Bible study session, a mission club meeting, or an apostolic action meeting. There is such a vast opportunity for any combination of practical gatherings for the spiritual and educational growth of the members while at the same time, members improve their openness to each other in ready communication as members of one family.

Fraternities should likewise urge their members to participate in regional and interregional meetings. Through these means, a Franciscan family consciousness is developed and the members benefit from an exchange of ideas on Franciscan gospel life, formation, promotion, and apostolic action. The Franciscan family concept can only be fully grasped by involvement in such meetings. A broader vision and understanding of Franciscanism is thus acquired by the members. Besides, these meetings assist members to experience Franciscan joy and brotherhood in action. The greetings of St. Francis "Pax et Bonum" (Peace and All Good to You) takes on flesh and blood.

The rule also calls upon the members of a fraternity to have a deep spiritual concern for sick and deceased members. Secular Franciscans should have a great solicitude for sick members by praying for them, visiting them, or writing to them. Any practical help extended to sick members is surely very much in order. By acting in this way, the members can be certain that they will abide in the spirit of the Gospel which St. Francis summed up in these words: "If a mother loves and cares for her child in the flesh, a friar (secular Franciscan) should certainly love and care for his spiritual brother (or sister) all the more tenderly (2 Rule 6)."

Each fraternity should make it a practice to prayerfully call to mind the deceased members at the November meeting each year. Practically all fraternities have a Holy Mass offered for each deceased member at the time of death, besides attending the wake and praying the rosary or some other para-liturgical prayers. Some fraternities enjoying a monthly fraternity Mass read the names of the deceased of the respective month at the memento for the dead.

All these various activities and responsibilities of a fraternity cannot be effectively carried out without financial means being available. Hence, the rule states: "Regarding expenses necessary for the life of the fraternity and the needs of worship, of the apostolate, and of charity, all the brothers and sisters should offer a contribution according to their means. Local fraternities should contribute to the expense of the higher fraternity councils;" namely, the regional, national, and international. The monies collected have always been known in Franciscan circles as the common fund because it is a pooling of material resources in the spirit of love for the sake of the common good. There are no dues in the Secular Franciscan Order, but a freewill offering given from a deep supernatural motive and an intelligent understanding that funds are required for the life and the work of the Franciscan Family. Hence, those who are unable to attend meetings for some legitimate reason should fulfill this special obligation by mailing in their excuse and offering.

It is the practice of many regional and national councils to call for a per capita offering from all of the members affiliated to them. Such per capita offerings are really not the responsibility of the individual members but of the common fund of the various fraternities. In this way, there is no direct burden on a member who is unable to meet such assessments.

SPIRITUAL ASSISTANCE AND VISITATION

Every fraternity needs healthy and sound spiritual assistance. Therefore, the rule states: "As a concrete sign of communion and coresponsibility, the councils on various levels, in keeping with the constitutions, shall ask for suitable and well prepared religious for spiritual assistance." When a Franciscan religious is not available, a council should see a Franciscan-minded diocesan priest or deacon for this purpose.

The spiritual, inspirational, and educational life of a fraternity benefits greatly from a capable spiritual assistant. It is the duty of the spiritual assistant to prepare and deliver a monthly Franciscan conference and be available for counseling. The spiritual assistant is by his very office a member of the council of the fraternity. In the council affairs, he contributes to the spiritual formation of officers and the liturgical and devotional life of the council and the fraternity. He is to guide the apostolic efforts of a fraternity that they are based on and carried out in a supernatural manner in accordance with the spirit of the Church and the Franciscan family. The spiritual assistant also represents the Church at all receptions, professions, jubilees, and other ecclesial functions.

It has always been the practice in every the Secular Franciscan Order to have a visitation of the various fraternities and councils annually or at least occasionally. The visitation of a fraternity or a council by some representative of the regional council and by the proper friar representative, has done much to unite fraternities, to inspire them, to bring about an understanding of the wider goals and programs, and to assist them in correcting some weaknesses.

The visitor formerly was always only a friar, the provincial spiritual assistant or some other friar delegated by him. The rule now asks that a second visitor be appointed, namely some Secular Franciscan. On this point, the rule reads: "To promote fidelity to the charism as well as observance of the rule and to receive greater support in the life of the fraternity, the minister or president, with the consent of the council, should take care to ask for a regular pastoral visit by the competent religious superiors as well as for a fraternal visit from those of the higher fraternities, according to the norm of the constitutions."

It is now the responsibility of each minister and council to request visitation. Necessarily, this need not be done each year, but a good leadership on the local level will recognize the wisdom of an annual visitation or visitation at reasonable intervals. This request is, of course, made to the regional council to which the fraternity is affiliated, and to the appropriate friar entity.

The pastoral visitor is the provincial spiritual assistant or his delegate. The pastoral visitor's responsibility is the spiritual liturgical, and devotional life of the fraternity. He looks for leadership in the spiritual assistant and the officers as it addresses the Franciscan and ecclesial dimensions of their duties. His visitation conference to all of the members is the highlight of his visit along with his personal contact with as many of the members as possible for private spiritual consultation.

The fraternal visitor is a Secular Franciscan from the council of the region or a Secular Franciscan can from another fraternity appointed by the minister of the regional council. It is the duty of the fraternal visitor to enliven the fraternal life of the fraternity, to strengthen the functioning of the officers, to discuss Franciscan family life, and inspire all of the members to appreciate their vocations, promote vocations, and help in any way to inject enthusiasm into the apostolic endeavors of the fraternity.

The two visitors form a complementary team for the well-being of any fraternity. They both wish to be available to all the members; and their duties, in some instances, can easily overlap.

From the above, you can readily see that these last articles of the rule contain many directives that are essential to the proper functioning of the Secular Franciscan Family.

Conclusion

T The "dynamic power of the Gospel," which is made present and effective through the text of the SFO Rule and through the lives of those who put it into practice, is the source, the end, and the energy for fulfilling the Franciscan charism in the Church and in the world.

It is the *source* of the Franciscan charism because the gospel way is the foundation on which this particular spiritual family has been built and the font out of which springs the Franciscans' careful attention to fidelity to the Church, change of heart, prayer, and the imitation of Mary.

It is the *end* of the Franciscan charism because, as the prologue of the rule indicates, this gospel way is the purpose for being Franciscan and for uniting the whole Franciscan Family together as an evangelized community and as an evangelizing force.

It is the *energy* for this Franciscan charism to be actualized because it provides the motivation and the means to embrace the gospel counsels in a secular way; to build a spirit of brotherhood within the SFO and throughout society; to assume responsible evangelizing action in public life, in the family or in nature, at all times bringing out justice and peace; and to take on the necessary responsibilities of service within fraternal life, whether in leadership, in formation, or in community participation.

The dynamic power of the Gospel is the basic core of Franciscan commitment because it is the power of a Person in whom "we live and move and have our being" (Acts 17:28): Jesus Christ himself. By profession of the Franciscan life and rule, a person is bound permanently to the Lord Jesus who gives the grounding for all meaning and effectiveness, who challenges his followers to achieve the goal of their existence, and who provides the inspiration and the example to accomplish all things in his Name and through his Way.

In all this, then, our lives are to echo the words of Celano spoken of Francis: "[His] highest intention, his chief desire, his uppermost purpose was to observe the holy Gospel in all things and through all things and, with perfect vigilance, with all zeal, with all the longing of his mind and all the fervor of his heart, 'to follow the teaching and the footsteps of our Lord Jesus Christ'" (1Cel 84).

BAF

Index

T

101